A LIFE ON THE SPECTRUM

Discovering Late in Life That I Have Asperger's Syndrome

Bill Klubeck

ISBN 978-0-578-25957-4   print
ISBN 978-0-578-25958-1   digital

Cover design by: Mikeyj007
Printed in the United States of America

DEDICATION

I'd like to dedicate this book to the following:

To my wife, Tammy, the love of my life and my "coach". She's been a loving, patient, and supportive partner and friend all these years. It was with her guidance that I discovered my true self, which gave me what I needed to write this book and start a new chapter in my life (pun fully intended).

To my kids, all five of them. God called me to be your dad. While I wasn't perfect, know that I did the best I could, and I love every one of you. I'm proud of you and can't wait to see what each one of you will do next.

To Dr. Kaarin, whose guidance and expertise made this book possible.

To all of my friends and family, who, without exception, have shown nothing but excitement and support for this endeavor. Thank you for your encouragement, I will always be there to do the same when you need it.

To my mechanics – the technical expertise, Yasmin and Mike, for helping fine tune the inside and providing a great paint job for the exterior, respectively.

To my God and my Father: thank you, Lord, for your strength and guiding Spirit. You've heard my prayers, been caring and patient in less than stellar times, and kept with me all along this journey. You've given me the inspiration for this book, and I cannot thank You enough for that.

"I will praise You, for I am fearfully and wonderfully made;
Marvelous are Your works, and that my soul knows very well."
Psalm 139:14

CONTENTS

DEDICATION...iii

FOREWORD vi

1 WHAT IS ASD? 1

2 NO FILTERS OR GATES 5

3 SENSORY OVERLOADS IN FULL FORCE 12

4 IT WASN'T ALL BAD... 19

5 WELL, *THAT* DIDN'T WORK OUT AS PLANNED........ 34

6 COMING OF AGE... 46

7 THINGS GET A LITTLE STRANGE 61

8 LITTLE DID I KNOW 78

9 LIFE SINCE THE DIAGNOSIS 84

10 PERSPECTIVES 88

A FINAL NOTE 91

FOREWORD

Imagine: you are a fairly successful adult, married with kids, maybe even starting to think about retirement, and you are met with a startling, life-changing discovery. You find out, late in life, that you suffer from a neurological disorder. And you didn't just get this condition; it's something that you were born with. You've had it your entire life.

While the news is startling, even troubling at first, you realize it's not a worst-case scenario. While it hasn't seriously affected you (that you can think of), as you look back over your life, all kinds of light bulbs start going off. You can see now, clear as a bell, why you acted a certain way in elementary school. Why you were so afraid of something as a young child. Why certain things confused and even upset you – things that everyone else seemed to take in stride.

As an adult, your childhood fears and anxieties seemed to be behind you and you took on life. You went to college or got a job after high school, maybe met the love of your life, got married and started settling down…but there were still some situations that left you feeling uncomfortable. Some interactions or day-to-day events seemed to upset you for no good reason. At times, your family maybe saw you as withdrawn or even short-tempered.

This is life with autism spectrum disorder, or ASD. The first chapter of this book will be talking about what that is. Most of us are probably familiar with the term, as it's much more common in the last twenty years than at any time since it's discovery. You may have a friend or family member who's on the spectrum. It's even possible that YOU could be. Whether you're reading this for yourself or someone else, I hope to provide some insights and anecdotal encouragement.

Writing this book is something I had to do. It started life as a blog post that I thought I could keep to the size of an article. Well, I was wrong about that. It quickly grew out of control and took on a life of its own. I've wanted to write a book since I was a kid, and it dawned on me…This is it. This story I'm trying to tell – this is my book.

So, this is my story, a memoir. I also hope it can serve as an aid to those who live with ASD. Whether you have a friend or family member who's on the spectrum, or if you suspect that you yourself are, or if you've been tested and diagnosed with ASD, then this book is for you. There's hope! If you're still struggling to accept the reality of this diagnosis, and if you are struggling with how to move on with life, keep reading.

"Bear one another's burdens, and so fulfill the law of Christ."
Galatians 6:2

PART 1: ASD DEFINED

1
WHAT IS ASD?

Autism spectrum disorder, or ASD, is a neurological condition that affects social and emotional development. It creates a neurodiverse condition where the brain is "wired differently" from that of a neurotypical one. I'll use these terms to describe people on the autism spectrum: ASD and ND (neurodivergent/neurodiverse), and those who are not, NT (neurotypical). The terms neurodivergent and -diverse refer to an individual and a group, respectively. These terms encompass a number of "brain differences", including cognitive and social learning as seen in ASD, but also include differences seen in ADD/ADHD and dyslexia.

Autism was first defined and diagnosed in 1943 by Austrian psychiatrist and physician Leo Kanner. He initially described autistic individuals as having an "anxiously obsessive desire for the maintenance of sameness." Along with this, Kanner believed autism was primarily an emotional condition that didn't affect an individual's ability to perceive and learn. It was first listed in the Diagnostic and Statistical Manual of Mental Disorders (DSM) 2nd edition, published in 1952, as a form of schizophrenia with behavioral and environmental causes.

The ideas behind its symptoms and origins have changed significantly since Kanner first described it. By the time DSM III was published in 1980, researchers had re-defined autism as a "pervasive developmental disorder" distinct from schizophrenia. Autism was noted to cause the patient to have little to no interest in other people, the inability or significantly impaired ability to communicate, and unusual responses to their surroundings. These traits were found to develop in patients within the first three years of life.

The DSM III was revised in 1987 to include a milder form of autism called Pervasive Developmental Disorder-Not Otherwise Specified (PDD-NOS) and while the term "spectrum" was not actually used, this revised definition reflected the understanding that autism was not a standalone condition, but a spectrum of conditions with varying degrees of severity that can present throughout life. Not long after, when the 4th edition of the DSM was published in 1994, it included the term "spectrum" in autism's definition, and added Asperger's disorder as a milder form of autism.

Asperger's disorder was defined just one year after Kanner had defined autism. Hans Asperger, an Austrian pediatrician and professor, saw behaviors in children that were similar to autistic tendencies, but with marked differences. Where autistic individuals were quite anti-social and self-isolating, those who had Asperger's syndrome wanted to socialize with others but were awkward and even inappropriate in their approach.

Another distinguishing factor is that patients with Asperger's have quite developed, even advanced, language and communication abilities. However, they lack the "common sense" factor for properly using their skills in normal social interactions. Their interests, and subsequently their conversations, tend to be very one-sided. Asperger's individuals might be taken as arrogant or even narcissistic, when actually there is no ill intent in their communication.

It's the discomfort and anxiety caused by interacting with others in a way that just doesn't come naturally, even as those with Asperger's get older. As one with the condition, I'll speak for myself: we just don't get it. To cope, we seek a place of comfort, and that's something and someone that we DO understand – us, ourselves.

It makes sense when you think about it. Generally, whenever any of us are in an awkward or stressful situation, we're looking for an escape. We want to lessen the bad feeling, so we flee. In social situations, NDs flee inward. Take it from one who knows…I never mean to be anti-social or self-absorbed. I want to reach out to others, listen to them, make them feel important and included in conversation. But the way my brain's wired, I can only take so much interaction before I start to turn inward because I just don't know how to keep a two-way interaction going.

At over fifty years old, you'd think I'd have figured it out by now. I can put on my "happy face" and fake it a lot of times, for a while. Other times, though, my natural mode of processing wins out and I'll either start talking too much about myself, or I just retreat.

This is also where a trait common to both autism and Asperger's comes into play: mind blindness. It is the inability to properly read others during social interaction – visual cues such as body language, facial expression, and verbal cues where the other person may be hinting at their desire to talk or to leave the conversation altogether.

Another ability Asperger identified is a very high intelligence, especially in one key interest area. This can be present in individuals with either autism or Asperger's syndrome. This high intelligence in one or a few key areas is similar to savant syndrome, and in some cases (such as the character "Rain Man", and his real-life inspiration), this can be a crossover condition.

Cognitive differences are also a distinguishing factor with people on the spectrum. We don't process information the same as an NT person. Some things come very quickly to us, much quicker than to NT people. Other things that NTs take for granted, we NDs stumble over time and again. This will be described more in the next chapter.

"But to do good and don't forget to communicate with others: for with such sacrifices God is pleased." Hebrews 13:16

2
NO FILTERS OR GATES

Research has found that a neurotypical brain has filters or gates that control the amount and intensity of input or stimuli that the brain receives at any given time. They allow a person to not get too overwhelmed if there are, say, multiple conversations going on in a group setting. They even help someone to function in the midst of chaos and disorganization. My wife, for example, is very good at tuning out background noise. To an ND individual, though, this can make others seem somewhat insensitive or inattentive.

Those on the spectrum don't have such filters or gates, or at least, they're not very well developed. We tend to hear, see, and smell everything at once, and with a much higher intensity than NT people. When we're in the midst of chaos – kids running around, dogs barking, any type of party or gathering – we get mentally rattled because we're receiving all of these fractured, disparate inputs at once, all at high intensity, and it's overwhelming.

One day I was riding with my wife in her car. She was playing a video on her phone, piping it through the car's sound system. It wasn't a music video, it was someone giving a talk. So, I focused on what the person was saying, because it was interesting and I wanted to process it. Whenever my wife would interject with a comment, I would immediately become flustered and have to grab the phone and pause the video.

I could not process both the speaker and my wife's comments simultaneously. They were both coming in at the same intensity, as disparate but equally intense inputs, causing neurological chaos in my head. Situations like this cause a mental and emotional overload, and my anxiety spikes. When this happens, I literally cannot think straight. It'll become hard to talk. The best way I've found to describe it is like mental suffocation. The brain just wants to shut down. This is what causes meltdowns and withdrawal of an ND person.

A meltdown, especially in a child, looks very much like a temper tantrum. However, the child has intention and control over their actions during a temper tantrum. It's a power play for control of a situation that they are dissatisfied with. An ASD child is simply overwhelmed mentally and emotionally and can't express him or herself properly, so they are literally blowing off steam because their head feels like it wants to explode. It's a reflex reaction, a fight or flight behavior that they have little to no control over.

The flight, or withdrawal, escape, et al, is the next logical and important step to an ND person suffering from sensory overload. I've felt this quite dramatically in crowded situations, such as large family gatherings or holiday shopping. The mental suffocation kicks in, and I just need to get out of there. It's a visceral response. I can't explain it, and I have little to no control over it.

Because of this inability to filter out multiple stimuli or dial down the intensity in which they're received, I really can't multi-task. I have to be single-minded in what I'm doing or thinking. In order to cope, I have to be very deliberate to block out everything else except what I'm focused on doing or thinking.

For example, I can NOT talk and drive at the same time. If I do, I will drift toward the conversation and allow my intuitive skills do the driving. This gets me down the road safely but does nothing for specific directions. If I'm engaged in conversation, I will miss turns, even well-known ones, almost every time.

Paul Micallef, one of my favorite YouTubers, has a channel called "Aspergers from the Inside". He compares his singular intensity to NT people this way: we all have a certain amount of mental energy that we burn throughout the day. For NT types, their filters and gates help manage their energy consumption as the day goes on. For those of us with ASD, and our single-minded intensity, we burn very bright, very fast. Meaning, we put everything we have into the one thing we're working on or thinking about. And then our bucket is empty, so we need to rest and recharge.

For a long time, I realized deep down that this was happening, but I didn't fully connect the need to rest during the day with expending most of my energy very quickly due to that ND singular intensity. I've always been a bit hyper, so I connected my need to rest more with physical exhaustion. But this makes sense when you think about it. When our brains are exhausted, it affects our physical well-being also. The brain doesn't want to command the body to do much when it's spent. It just wants to shut off and recharge.

We've all likely experienced the opposite of this. At night, when we've been physically active during the day and our bodies are tired, but our minds are alert and awake, it's nearly impossible to fall asleep. The body wants to shut down and recharge, but consciousness is more dictated by the brain than the body. If you're lying in bed, weary from a hard day's work but your mind is spinning, you're probably not getting to sleep any time soon.

One positive aspect of being hyper and having a singular, high-speed brain is the ability to pick up on details very quickly. Tests for the autism spectrum look for attention to detail, and not a general "big picture" view. This threw me off, because I've always thought one of my strengths was the ability to see the big picture, a bigger vision of a given situation.

I never thought of myself as someone who gets fixated on details. After some recent research into personality typing (there will be more on this in the Final Note at the end of the book), I've found that my natural personality type strongly lends itself to being intuitive and getting a big-picture view, and basing decisions and conclusions on that. Thus, I've got a serious dichotomy inside my head: my natural personality leads me to be intuitive and big-picture minded; my Asperger's causes me to see and hear everything. This applies mostly to concrete things, while the intuition applies more to the abstract or theoretical.

It's a double-edged sword – blessings and curses, combined. My ASD brain is in high gear most of the time, uber-analyzing one or two things at a time. I can learn new skills very fast, if I concentrate on one or two aspects at a time. The negative part of learning new things quickly with a brain that runs best in high gear is that I can easily become bored. As much as an Aspie likes routine, schedule and sameness, I need to remain challenged intellectually.

Early on in my career, I got derailed from manufacturing engineering, which I went to college for and enjoyed, into quality engineering. This was not by choice, but I needed a job, so I took it. And, I decided I was going to be good at what I did, so I could move up and get raises to support my growing family.

So, when I started a new role as a supplier quality engineer, I dove into it and just tore it up for the first several months. I wanted to learn and do as much as I could, as quickly as I could. The reason for this was twofold: one, as I mentioned, I wanted to do a good job and look good for management, so that I'd get raises. But second, and this was more subconscious at the time, it was to establish routine and sameness for my ASD brain.

A new job is exciting and challenging, and there are a lot of new things thrown at you to learn. I enjoyed the intellectual stimulation, but it was also stressful for me because of the new and unexpected. Surprises can be very stressful for the ND person and it can ruin their whole day. We are very linear, literal thinkers when it comes to communication, planning and schedules.

With any new job now, especially this far along in my career, I can usually master it pretty quickly; within a couple of months or less. Again, this sets me up for intellectual failure; because, once I've mastered it and there are no more surprises, I'm then no longer intellectually stimulated. You've probably felt this way, going into work, day after day, doing the same old thing. It can get boring. To my ASD brain, it's the extreme – like, five times worse. I will sometimes sit at my desk and just be going crazy in my head, wanting to get up and run out of there. I'll sit there wondering what's become of my life.

This is a big reason why I keep a journal and write in it daily. It's cathartic; I'm able to vent all this steam into words on the page, to help keep my sanity. In general, it's hard for people with ASD to hold down a job. The reasons are typically due to sensory overload (office or shop settings with bright lights and loud or unfamiliar noises); inability to interact well with others (social anxiety); and not being able to figure out or complete the work fast enough.

While these have bothered me some, they haven't been show-stoppers. Years of coping and masking without realizing what I'm doing have kind of numbed the senses a bit and taught me to deal with low to mid-intensity situations. The biggie has been the conflict between needing sameness and routine while remaining intellectually challenged.

I've worked hard over the years to stay on course with the jobs that I've held. I try to make improvements in the activities or the role itself, more to grant that intellectual challenge than to shine the spotlight on myself for accolades or awards.

Not that the social interactions haven't caused me problems – they have. I'm sure that I've lost two jobs based on what I'd call inappropriate interaction with my boss. In one case, we were getting along just fine. I'd recently had a great review from him, and got a small raise. A couple of months had passed, and we struck up a conversation involving his salary. This gave me the bright idea to go in and ask him for a raise, beyond what I'd received during my review.

I'm still not sure what happened. I think it was a combination of my approach, and him as a person. I did not get the raise. Instead, I got blacklisted. He proceeded to make my life miserable. When he reacted completely opposite of what I expected, I felt ostracized. I went to a dark, lonely place and shut down. He demanded that I perform better than I had been – more work in less time. Instead, I did less. My productivity and motivation were shot. It was only a matter of time. I was demoted from manager to engineer, and eventually let go.

The very next job that I got, I vowed that I wouldn't let my motivation or productivity suffer. It happened to be my former employer's rival. I worked hard. So hard, in fact, that I ticked off my boss there. I was doing TOO good, and it was making him look bad. He finally took me to lunch one day and threatened my job. If I didn't dumb it down, he was going to find a reason to get rid of me. I couldn't believe it.

This time, instead of succumbing to depression and just giving up, I got mad. I wasn't going to let this knucklehead pull this on me. But I knew I couldn't stay there, either. I mellowed out just enough to get by, and started looking for another job. I was never happier to hand someone my two-week notice.

Along the way there's been some company politics – I can't stand insincere people who're only interested in their own success.

I'm a transparent person and very passionate about what I do. This is also the Idealist in me; the personality type thing again.

Meaning is important to me. Really, the best part of my job, the part I can naturally do very well, is diplomacy. This primarily involves talking to customers who have a problem or complaint with our product. Because I enjoy edifying and encouraging people, I can put them at ease and my follow up is at or above their expectation level.

So, I get by and do the best I can with what I've got. But that still doesn't change the fact that I would love to find more intellectual stimulation, or do something with a greater meaning.

I've discussed what ASD is – its origins, the different types that all fall under the same spectrum. I've described some of the "symptoms" or characteristics a neurodiverse, or person on the autism spectrum, might display. And I've covered briefly how some of those characteristics have affected me in social and career settings. This is just a sampling. Now let's look at how ASD affected an unsuspecting child.

PART 2: ASD LIFE AS A CHILD, K-12TH GRADE

3
SENSORY OVERLOADS IN FULL FORCE

I was born and lived the first few years of my life in suburban Detroit, Michigan. I was the second of three kids. As a toddler, I'd already displayed some unusual traits. I remember being either captivated or terrified by different loud noises. For example, I distinctly remember a work crew coming with a chipper to cut down and dispose of an old tree in our front yard. My sensitivity to loud noises came on early; but, if I found the source of the noise fascinating, such as the chipper, I couldn't help but stand and watch it work. I still have fleeting memories of this; standing in our living room, watching rapt out the front window, terrified and fascinated at the same time.

Each time a worker put a limb or big chunk of tree in the machine's spinning mouth, I'd jump, and early on, I would run away each time. But as the work kept up and I realized that a) it wasn't going to get any louder, and b) I wasn't in any immediate danger, I became more and more fixated by the nature of the thing. This fascination over fear would soon present itself in what became a decades long love of a great mechanical behemoth. I'll get into that in more detail later.

There were plenty of loud noises that completely freaked me out and shut me down. Motorcycles, for example. The big, rumbling Harley-types were NOT my thing. Another distinct memory as a toddler was when a neighbor had just such a bike, and he sat in the driveway one day revving it up, over and over. I stood in my yard, hands clamped over my ears, crying and screaming bloody murder, too paralyzed to run away. The neighbor was looking at me and just grinning at me in the midst of my terror and pain. My mom had to come out and lead me away, giving dirty looks to the obnoxious reprobate.

Although, I do remember being in nursery school, and doing okay. I never got stressed or overloaded when my mom dropped me off. Most other parts of my early childhood were fairly normal, but this would change dramatically when I was four years old and my dad got a new job, when we moved to our second and final home.

I'd lived the first four years of my life in a busy, metropolitan area with grandparents, aunts and uncles, and cousins not far away. We lived in a small but tidy – and modern – ranch house. Now we were moving 200 miles away to Cadillac, Michigan. New town, new home, and a new neighborhood with all new kids. I would also be starting kindergarten in this new place.

All of my sameness and routine was ripped up and replaced, and I hated it. It was a small, slow-paced town, and our house was a dark, two-story affair that was at least a hundred years old. It was rickety and creaky, and made noises at night when I was trying to go to sleep. I complained a lot about missing my cousins and being away from the action and busyness of suburban Detroit. I would literally dream at night of being back there, or at least moving our old house to Cadillac to live in.

And while I was fine at the nursery school I attended in suburban Detroit, I hated kindergarten at my new school from day one. My mother would have to drag me in there, literally kicking and screaming. Little did we know then, but I was having an ASD meltdown. Sensory overload, too many brand-new stimuli for my brain to handle at once. I had also developed quite a phobia to bathrooms, toilets in particular. I'm not sure why, it may have been the time that I plugged our toilet up by throwing a paper cup into it, only to have my dad come home after work and unplug it, mumbling and swearing under his breath the whole time. At any rate, an irrational but very real (to me) fear.

So, I didn't like going to the bathroom in strange places, and especially in this new school that terrified me. This led to a worse situation where I'd sit on the floor during circle time, and wet myself because I didn't want to step foot in the bathroom. It was a classic ASD sensory problem.

I started to grow out of the toilet phobia after kindergarten and by first grade could use the bathrooms in the hall. It also didn't take me long at all to figure out the path to walk to school in the morning. My mom walked it with me a couple of times – it was a straight shot, four blocks up Hersey Street. You couldn't help but run right into it. And yes, back then, we walked ourselves to school in first and second grade. Well, I walked myself *to* school.

Here's where another ASD weirdness kicked in. When I'd get done at the end of the day, I'd walk to the intersection where I'd have to cross, at Lester and Hersey streets. As luck would have it, my brother was usually the crossing guard there. And I would freeze, just lock up. I couldn't do it. I couldn't remember the way home, the same four block straight shot that I took to get there. I'd start crying and freaking out. My brother had to ask permission to leave his post for a few minutes, and he'd walk me the first block or two, and then I'd be okay.

You'd think after the first time or two, I'd have gotten the hang of it. But no, I remember it took several times of this for me to finally get it. Why was this? Why could I walk *to* school alone, fine and confident, but at the end of the day, I could not for the life of me handle the return trip? The only thing I can figure is the very linear, single path method that an ASD brain works. My mom hadn't walked the return trip with me, so it didn't imprint on my brain the same way.

Socially, I didn't fit in very well. I was an awkward kid with big front teeth, so invariably ended up getting picked on for being "buck-toothed". I was terribly shy, which is pretty normal with kids on the spectrum. So, making friends was hard. I was very sensitive to being picked on and bullied, and I got into more fights than I made friends. The fights were usually with the same two kids, Rick and Bob. Both farm boys, both would whip my butt every time. When I got the chance, I would lash out at the rare kid that came along who was less fortunate than me.

This, one day, came back to haunt me. There was a new family that had moved to the area, and their kids – two sisters, and a brother in my grade – all came to our school and were all less fortunate than most of us. The brother quickly became a target of persecution. You would've thought that, after everything I'd been through, I'd have some empathy for this poor kid. But no, this was my chance to level the field. I could show the few friends I had that I was cool too, and I could pick on someone too, because I thought that's what I needed to do to fit in.

One day while this poor kid was starting to walk home, my friends and I were in the front parking lot of the school, yelling at him and taunting him. He was yelling back, so I upped the ante – I picked up a stone and threw it at him. And, as luck would have it, it hit him…right in the side of the head. He immediately grabbed his head and cried in pain. You know those times when you're feeling like a big man, and then you're suddenly deflated to about one inch tall? That was one of those times. His older sister was crossing guard nearby, and saw the whole thing.

She reported me to the office, and the next day, in the middle of class, she came walking in and spoke to the teacher. The teacher had me come up front, and this girl escorted me to the office. How frightening, and humiliating at the same time! I don't remember the punishment – I'm sure it involved apologizing to him – but I do remember getting a stern talking to from the principal and a couple of other teachers in the conference room.

The next year, on the first day of school, I walked into my third-grade classroom. We were all kind of milling about, talking, and waiting for the teacher to get us all organized, when I felt like I'd been punched in the gut. In walked a new kid, Robert. Robert was the spitting image of the boy who I had beaned with a stone last year.

Remember, I'd hit that poor kid right in the side of the head. Well, Robert, as this kid's doppelganger, had a big brown birthmark – it looked like a big oval, almost an inch in diameter – on his right temple…looking just like a big brown bruise, where a stone might've hit. They say God has a sense of humor. This was Him definitely pulling one over on me. I learned my lesson and I never tried to bean anyone ever again.

As dysfunctional as childhood seemed, I had a solid family life. My older brother had joined the Boy Scouts, and my dad was a Scout leader, so I joined the Cub Scouts and followed into the fold. I learned a lot of my practical life lessons from my dad. One thing he taught me, both in scouts and at home, was how to leave as small a footprint behind as possible. Whether you were going to make food and eat in the kitchen, or wash up in the bathroom, or make camp in the woods, always clean up after yourself. Leave a place as good or better than you found it. I don't know why, but this particular piece of advice stuck with me.

Being around a bunch of other kids in scouts, it didn't take too long for one of the darker sides of my ASD to come shining through. It all came to a head one time: the awkwardness of social interactions, and the anxiety they caused; the anger and hurt of being picked on or excluded from the group at school; and the hyper-intensity I possessed.

Not yet old enough to be a Boy Scout but tagging along with dad and older brother, we went on a weekend camping trip. During this trip, the "White Tornado" was born. And thankfully it blew itself out pretty quickly.

The hyper-intensity sometimes translated into an overall hyperactivity; I would zip around everywhere. The "White Tornado" nickname was dubbed by some of the older boys, because I was wearing a white sailor's hat like Gilligan and zipping around the campground. The aforementioned angst from social rejection flared up, and I started flailing at the occasional older Scout, and at first, they thought this was hilarious.

But then, fed by their encouraging laughter, and fueled by blind anger at always being the spastic little brother who got picked on, I went nuts. I literally became a little white tornado, arms extended and spinning furiously as I dove into first one and then another older Scout, swinging away blindly. My funny little act suddenly became a very obnoxious, injurious and senseless fit. It had been my way, my *only* way of being the center of attention – social anxiety mixed with a meltdown. ASD at its worst.

At that time, my emotions were just as intense as my sensory perceptions. If I was happy, I was elated. If I was sad, it was the end of the world. I can remember one time, I was probably nine or ten years old, standing in our dining room looking towards everyone in the living room, and I was having a bit of a meltdown. Over what, I cannot remember, but I do remember my parents' reaction to it.

They made casual remarks about me having either angst or angina…I can't remember clearly which word it was. The former certainly fit me; the latter could've very well been perceived as my problem. But that shows the extent of their insight at that time, the mid-1970s, of what Asperger's disorder looked like. They thought I was having general anxiety, or a pediatric heart condition.

All in all, my early childhood years were a pretty tumultuous time.

"These things I have spoken to you, that in me you might have peace. In the world there will be trouble; but be of good cheer, for I have overcome the world." John 16:33

4
IT WASN'T ALL BAD

I grew up in the 1970s and 80s with parents – and a community at large – that didn't really know much about ASD, much less recognize it and provide help. This actually had its upsides. For one thing, it toughened me up. Instead of a culture of labels and identities, I was just a spaz. I was told to knock it off, get over it, shape up. While you may think this is terribly harsh and insensitive, it was really what I needed to get moving in life. Sometimes tough love is the best kind.

My family was a little different. My mom and dad loved each other, although they didn't seem to know it half the time. There were warm and caring moments between them, and there were also some pretty loud arguments. They came from a generation that didn't believe in divorce. Both of my grandfathers died when my parents were young; I never knew them.

With an older brother and younger sister, our sibling rivalries flowed downhill: my brother would pick on me, and I couldn't do much about it, so I trickled it down to Becky. But my brother and sister got along just fine. They would say that we had a dysfunctional home life. Looking back with what I know now, it wasn't that bad. We weren't abused, and our parents didn't drink or neglect us. But I can say for sure that ASD definitely played a part in my upbringing. And not just with me. I'm 99% sure that my brother is on the spectrum, and I'm pretty sure my dad was too. ASD has genetic roots, and it runs in boys more than in girls.

My dad could be scary, flying off the handle at little things. He never raised a hand to any of us, but he would scare us just the same with his rages. Face and neck purple, veins bulging. I think something would cross his wires, so to speak, and he would have a meltdown, which would be taken out on us. I know he loved us, which is what I think kept him from being violent with us.

When a person with ASD is melting down, it's not like they mean to lash out at a particular person. They just want the mental chaos to stop. They're upset at all the loud white noise in their head. I know; I'm still learning how to reign in the chaos and disperse the white noise without going off. Now, if the source of the chaos happens to be one of my family, then yes, I might unload on them a bit. Although I don't turn purple with veins bulging, but I do get a little loud sometimes, and that's what my dad was doing.

We would do or say things that didn't line up with his particular linear thinking, and it would create mental havoc. Remember, ASD brains can be very smart and very fast – but only with one thing at a time. And with no filters to blot out the background sensory inputs, it quickly and significantly disrupts our train of thought.

All the same, though, we didn't realize any of this at the time, and so we just thought our dad was often angry and our mom was an emotional wreck because of it. Needless to say, this galvanized both of my siblings to not want to have kids of their own. My brother said it outright once – he didn't want to chance being like our dad to his own kids. I never held that fear; somehow, I always knew that whatever circumstances you're raised in, you are still your own person, and you can make yourself whatever you want to be.

How true that would become later in my life. Despite the bad times, my dad taught me a lot of good life lessons that I've tried to pass on to my own kids. Never stop learning, no matter how old you get. Do what you love, don't chase money or status. And the classic, you can do anything you put your mind to.

I always respected my dad, even when he was angry. He had a rough upbringing; both my parents did. He was the youngest of three kids, along with my uncle Pete and aunt Sonia. Their dad died when he was only seven years old, and they grew up poor in Detroit. My uncle Pete was a big hulk of a guy. He worked in construction, and went overseas during World War II. As kids, Pete picked on my dad relentlessly. My little old grandma Mary used to get on a chair and whack Pete with a broom when he was in trouble. Big old uncle Pete, fought in the war, but took his beating from Ma when he messed up.

My dad was sick a lot as a kid. I don't remember all the stuff wrong with him, but the doctors told him he wasn't going to live past eighteen. He beat those odds and met my mom at work in his early 30s. They got married and raised a family. He died in 2015 at eighty-seven years old.

My mom was thirteen years younger than my dad, and she had her own set of issues growing up. Mom never liked the sport of hockey, so when my oldest son Troy and I started playing, she wasn't all that excited about it. She never told us when we were younger, but I found out later that it was because of her parents. They liked to watch the Red Wings when she was growing up. And they liked to drink. So, in the middle of a game, after downing several beers each, with Gordie Howe probably walloping one of his opponents in the corner, my grandparents would beat the stuffing out of each other in a beer and hockey-induced frenzy.

My maternal grandfather passed away at work one day. He was a refrigerator repairman, and a unit he was working on was leaking freon gas. It poisoned him, and he never came home. My mom was seventeen at the time. This was obviously tough on both my grandma and my mom. I think my mom needed stability, and was very happy when she became Mrs. Klubeck.

Despite the fights and yelling in our home when I was young, we had our good times too. We went on family trips and vacations. Holidays, especially Christmas, were always memorable – and not just because of the presents. For those few weeks leading up to Christmas, the whole atmosphere in our house was magical. We always watched the Charlie Brown Christmas special. My parents would go out and get a live tree, and it was a family tradition to decorate it together. And then, in the evenings after the tree was properly put up, Mom and Dad would dim the lights, and then light a few candles, and the tree. They would play Christmas carols on our stereo. And I can remember laying on the living room floor, at peace, feeling the magic of the atmosphere, looking up at the tree.

I was raised to believe in God, and I am a born-again Christian. I grew up in a Catholic home, but I long ago left the church to pursue and expand my spiritual walk. I've had a strong connection with God since I was a young boy; He spoke to me directly once.

I can still remember it, to this day. I was about seven or eight years old, and I was standing in our living room, facing toward my father's chair and the window next to it. I don't remember what else I'd been thinking about at that moment, but I remember stopping and, as clear as a bell, a soft voice in my head said, "You're going to grow up, get married, and have a big family." It wasn't a directive; it sounded more like a prediction. I took it as a mission.

The reason that was so significant is because of how my family ended up growing up – my brother and sister, that is. As I mentioned, my brother never married or had any kids, and my sister married, but her husband already had children of his own, so they never had any kids. I am the lone offspring of my father to continue our Klubeck lineage.

But that moment, when I was given that message, stuck with me. I knew it had significant meaning, and wasn't just a passing thought of my own. It gave me peace because I knew God was watching over me. In the midst of a confusing and sometimes painful childhood, I could rest assured that my future was secure in the hands of a Father who would never become irrationally angry at me. This Father would always take care of me, as long as I trusted in Him.

Like all people with ASD, I definitely had a few very strong interests, and it was during my elementary years that I really engrossed myself in those interests. While I did have friends and we played together sometimes, I was also fine on my own, doing whatever it was that captivated me at the moment. Probably my strongest passion while growing up was a love of trains and railroading.

Trains are a common fixation for people on the spectrum. The fact that they run on organized schedules, and run on a pre-set track system, makes them very controlled and organized. Routine, organization and controlled surroundings are big pluses in an ASD person's life. There's also the variety of models, sizes and so on of both engines and cars.

I can remember getting books from the library on the many different types and sizes of diesel locomotives, and knowing – by memory – their horsepower and torque ratings by model and type. For me, there was also just this undefinable attraction to form. I just liked how trains, especially diesel locomotives, looked. And the sheer power they contained.

The fact that this behemoth could pull dozens and dozens of freight cars, each one weighing an average of 30 tons empty; a full 130 tons when loaded. That's incredible when you think about it.

Most freight trains you see have two engines up front, themselves each weighing about 150 tons.

Each locomotive produces between 4,000 and 6,000 horsepower; and, while powered by a huge diesel engine, actually have electric drive systems. The diesel engine is used to produce electric power via onboard generators, which then power the electric drive systems in each set of wheels.

The reason is because of the tremendous amount of torque needed to pull such weight. Gasoline engines excel at horsepower, which translates to speed but not a lot of pulling power. Diesels have higher torque and less horsepower, and don't rev as high as gas engines. Electric motors are even higher into the torque curve. So, for example, a large GE locomotive that produces 4,000 HP will produce at least 30,000 lb-ft of torque.

And that's probably far more than you wanted to know about railroading. As you can see, even in my fifties and having long ago shrugged off my acute affinity for trains, I still find them fascinating. But I get just as annoyed as you when I get stuck at a railroad crossing on my way to work in the morning.

Beyond railroading, I loved bike riding. I was always a wanderer, and my bike meant freedom. I could go nearly anywhere on it, and it was great. I wasn't always happy at home, with parents who didn't fully understand me and an older brother who enjoyed tormenting me. I'd go off on my own to the near, and far reaches of Cadillac, just to be alone with my thoughts.

It didn't take long for both of these interests, bike riding and railroading, to find a way to merge. As I got to be around eleven or twelve years old, I'd ride further from home, exploring the boundaries. I eventually made it one day to the north end of town, where the Michigan Northern and Ann Arbor railroads had a shared yard. Here, there were often two or three locomotives sitting idle.

One Saturday, I worked up the nerve and, carefully looking around to make sure no one was nearby watching, I climbed up into the cab of one of these slumbering giants. Remember, this was the late 1970s – there was no locking things up, no security cameras. I was free to sit in the driver's seat and live my dream...my imagination flew as I was the engineer of a real locomotive.

Another passion from youth to present day is books. Reading, and eventually writing, became my escape. I don't have a creative genius inside of me, but I still love putting words to the page. When I was in sixth grade, I went to a Young Author's weekend workshop. It was great. We learned about different types of books and writing styles. I came back from that fired up and determined to be an author someday. It took a while, but some day is finally here.

When home video games made their debut, I was hooked. I was first introduced to the Atari 2600 system at my cousin's house in Westland. Yet another reason why I hated living in Cadillac and pined for the days of suburban Detroit – living in a big city equated to having the coolest stuff.

Some of us might still remember the Atari. By today's standards, it's prehistoric. At that time, though, as a twelve-year-old, it was magic. I had odd jobs mowing lawns and delivering newspapers, and this was my first saving and investment opportunity. My parents never spent a ton on us, so I worked and saved up the $200 it cost at the time for a new Atari 2600 game system.

At about this same time, personal home computers came on the market. Apple had released the very first offering in 1976, followed shortly by the Radio Shack TRS-80 in 1977. Not long after that,

Commodore began releasing their models, which were more compact and affordable. They came with no monitor; they hooked up to your TV. So, a few years after saving for the family video game system, I again worked my tail off to save up another $200 and buy the family's first home computer – a Commodore 64.

I definitely had a work ethic at a young age, and I wasn't afraid to work hard and save my money. I was a spender, though – still am – and I have to be careful not to overdo it. I attribute this to the hyper-focus that most people with ASD have. We are very good at one thing at a time. Our single-minded intensity is generally unmatched. And it was through these things – my intense interest in railroading, bike riding, video games and computing – that I was able to express myself. These were my identity, and I was comfortable there. I had a lot of energy and desire to do and try things, so when I was tired of the more relaxing pursuits, I'd go burn off some of that energy by working at or on something.

I didn't often sit and feel sorry for myself or play the victim. I strove to make myself better. I coped and masked and mimicked to get along socially as best I could. I tried to minimize the anxiety and hurt of not fitting in. I was never cool, and I was often picked on. It drove my self-esteem into the gutter. As a kid from elementary through high school, I had almost zero self-confidence. But I didn't let it ruin me. Eventually it galvanized me, and I would make some very serious, solid life choices when I became a young adult – choices that moved me forward, not languishing in the past.

Even though I'd sometimes lash out at the occasional, unsuspecting kid to blow off steam, I really did have a lot of empathy for others who were downtrodden. Empathy is not a trait usually associated with those on the spectrum. A neurodivergent person, who's socio-emotional sensitivity and development are not in line with neurotypical people, can even develop empathy when they've been through a severe or repeated trial.

When you get ostracized and persecuted a lot, you tend to take pity on those around you in similar situations. I found this to be mostly true once I got into high school. In elementary school, as young children, we really don't know any better and our minds are still in development. I do remember understanding when others would hurt me or my friends, and I'd feel emotional pain from that.

Because of how our brains are wired for social interaction, there tends to be a lot of inward focus. An ASD person can often be seen as arrogant or narcissistic because of their focus on self. We often don't converse well – when you do finally get us to engage and start talking, we'll dominate a conversation into a monologue about our interests. When we are quiet while someone else is speaking, we often appear bored or distracted, or may even walk away.

This isn't narcissism out of conscious arrogance; it's simply how we sense and perceive others around us. Because we're very awkward around others, and interacting causes anxiety, we compensate by talking about the one thing we know best – our interests. When that's not happening, we're stuck in an uncomfortable situation that we want to get out of. We're generally unsure of how to respond to the input we're receiving from others, and often when we respond to it, it might come across as nonsensical, or even offensive. So, we remain quiet, until we get an opportunity to talk, and then it's straight to the comfort zone – me and my interest.

Once I got to middle school, it was a completely different story. Middle school was – and always will be – a socio-emotional slaughterhouse. Middle school is the worst time of childhood, even if you're neurotypical, because of the developmental stages at that age. Entering the teenage years, as puberty is hitting, everything's a mess. Hormone levels are spiking or all over the place, and our physical bodies are growing like crazy.

We're going from children to mini-adults almost overnight. It really messes with the emotional state of mind of even the most stoic of people. Now, imagine being a socio-emotional mess with ASD, who likes calm and routine, who likes their own interests and not much else; imagine this child being suddenly thrust into this new, hostile environment.

I stood out like a sore thumb – thick plastic teardrop-framed glasses, big front teeth, bowl-type haircut, and a big blue oversized old coat that looked like it belonged in the back of a second-hand shop. On my very first day of middle school, I was assaulted in front of everyone when two thugs threw me to the ground and gave me a "red belly". One held me down while the other lifted my coat and shirt, and open-palm slapped my stomach until it was bright red. It doesn't cause much physical damage, but it stings and it's mortifying. This sort of persecution continued, off and on, even into high school.

Ah, the emotional, hormonal upheaval that is middle school life. Early adolescence, in all its gloriously gory reality. Trying to find your place in social circles, trying to fit in and get along. Trying not to look or sound stupid, trying not to get laughed at. All that, times ten. Imagine being socio-emotionally impaired and trying to navigate the highly populated minefield of middle school. It was the worst time of my life, period.

And then there was Cathy. I thought I'd died and gone to Heaven. If ever there was a bright spot during those dark, turbulent times, it was her. I'd had a crush or two in elementary school, but nothing could've prepared me for the emotional smackdown that Cathy would lay on me. Imagine, after the very first morning, just arrived on school grounds, getting humiliated in front of everyone by the seventh grade's main two thugs, and then going in to homeroom and sitting in a four-person group with the most beautiful girl you've ever seen.

I forgot all about Calvin and Jerry and my stinging redbelly. I was in love. But of course, she would hardly pay me any mind. Oh, I was amusing to her, but that was it. She never had any serious feelings for me. I'd ask her to go with me about once a week. I even rode out to her house on the north edge of town, had her come to the door, to ask her to go with me. I'm sure she was a little annoyed, but she smiled and played it off as nicely as she could. She ended up dating Mark through most of middle school. Mark was a couple notches higher on the social ladder, and knew how to handle social interaction. I didn't stand a chance.

I was already awkward and geeky, but usually tried to be friendly and outgoing. After going through the hell that was middle school, I became a serious introvert. I just turned inward. I didn't want to reach out to anyone. People didn't understand me, so they didn't like me. But – I knew myself, and I was okay with that, so I began an off- and on-again life in my own head.

That pretty much defined my life for the next couple of years, being picked on by bullies, laughed at by the girls, and heartbroken at the girl I could never have. I remember walking to school dances, in the vain hope that she would finally notice me, and finally come to her senses and see that I was a really nice guy, just a little awkward; well, *quite* socially awkward. And emotionally; well, yeah. When I liked a girl, I LOVED her. I was head over heels, all in. By the eighth grade I was ready to take the vows. I was easily, and often, deeply hurt. There was a LOT of emotional turmoil in those years.

High school wasn't much better. Cathy moved away at the end of eighth grade. When I was a sophomore, there was another girl, Kim, that I had a crush on. She barely noticed me, of course. And there was yet another bully, Jim, in biology class. Things finally started to ease up when I became an upper classman.

One of the best things I did to become a more confident, independent person was join Junior Achievement in my junior year of high school. JA is a junior business training system for school-age kids. In my day, it was only available for high-schoolers. We met in the evening at the school, in the shop classes, and we formed little companies. We had adults who would advise us, but otherwise they let us run the show. We had to come up with our company name, logo, and appoint positions – Presidents and VPs, and other kids to do the work. We had to pick a product to either make or buy and re-sell. There were four or five companies total in our school.

The girl who started as our company president ended up quitting early on due to other school social obligations. And somehow, I was chosen to replace her. Me, picked to be the president of our company: White Pine Industries. I couldn't believe it. I'd never been picked to be first, or even second, in much of anything before.

We didn't take the easy route, either. We didn't buy and resell yo-yos or other gadgets like some groups did; we chose to make tip-ups. Tip-ups are a kind of fishing pole used for ice fishing. Since Cadillac is built around two lakes, Cadillac and Mitchell, ice fishing was and still is a huge part of life there.

We were a hit. We came in first place at the end-of-year competition for most sales. There was a big awards dinner; it was great. Around school in general, I was a nobody. I was someone to be either picked on or pitied. But in JA, I was a somebody. I'd taken our company to the top, and it felt good to be on top for once.

JA was directly responsible for *the* big event that really opened me up and brought me out of my Asperger's-induced shell. During the summer between my junior and senior years, there was a national Junior Achievement Leadership conference that was held on the campus of Indiana University. It lasted several days, and it was glorious.

There were hundreds of kids there. We bunked in a couple of the empty dorms. There were workshops and activities every day, and we also had some free time to just relax. Most of the trip, I did keep to myself pretty much. I had enough social anxiety around my own high school, with kids I mostly knew. Now I was thrown in with hundreds of strangers from around the country. The glory was tempered a bit by apprehension.

The best part, though, was the big event on the last night of the conference. There was a dance. Now, dances and me never got along well. I walked myself to many of them in middle school, just to gaze at the girl I loved while she danced and snuggled with her boyfriend. I'd stay a little while and then inevitably I'd walk home sad and brokenhearted all over again.

But this dance was different. I went "stag," which several of the guys were talking about like it was the coolest thing to do: go "stag". It just meant you didn't have a date and you were going alone, or with some other guy friends. I spotted a pretty girl who was also alone, and asked her if she wanted to dance. She said yes, and we went out for a not-too-slow dance. It was nice. She was bored, said thanks and walked away. Well, I got my very first dance in. If nothing else happened, the night was a success.

But something else did happen. One of my friends was hanging out with a girl, and she had a friend. Her friend was kind of cute – not entirely to my liking, but she was nice. She smiled and made friendly conversation, so I didn't have to work that hard. We danced a few times and by then it was getting late.

I rode the shuttle bus back to the girls' dorm with her. When we got out, she stopped and turned to me, looking up. I think she might've even said, "Well?" So, I bent down and we kissed. It went on for what seemed like a long time. I looked, and her eyes were closed and she was clearly enjoying the moment. I wasn't sure what to do next, and I didn't want it to go any farther than the kiss, so I broke it off and said, "I should be getting back. Good night." And that was it. She stood there looking at me, perplexed and I think a little frustrated as I walked away. Actually, I floated away. I was on cloud nine. I had my first kiss, and she didn't yell "Eww!" or run away.

Junior Achievement was very good to me. It gave me a club to belong to when I didn't fit in anywhere else. It highlighted my talents, and I felt a real sense of worth because of it. It brought me out of my shell socially, and helped me learn to interact with different kinds of people, even ones I didn't know.

Later on, after I'd graduated college and was working for a small manufacturer in Grand Rapids, I got a chance to give back to JA. Our VP of finance was very involved with the local JA program and was always hitting up coworkers to help out and volunteer. I was more than happy to oblige. By then, the program formats had changed significantly. They still had the after-school mini-companies for the high school kids, but now there were in-class programs for kids down to elementary level. So, instead of being an advisor to kids who were forming their own company, I got a mini curriculum – an extended lesson plan, really. It was broken into sections that I would teach to kids in 30 to 45-minute sessions, twice a week.

It was a blast. My first venture into teaching JA was a class of troubled inner-city boys, seventh and eighth grade, who'd been shuttled into what was basically a detention class. They had a petite, almost frail looking girl for a teacher. I immediately thought, "What did I get myself into?" But the teacher was tough; she was kind but firm, and she wasn't afraid of those kids. And they knew it. They knew she cared about them, and whatever they'd done, whatever they were like outside of that classroom, they were good kids in that classroom. They were a riot. I didn't expect much interaction with them, but for the most part, they were pretty engaged when I was there. It was something different; I broke up the classroom monotony.

I also taught a couple of elementary classes, fourth and sixth grades. By then, I didn't mind getting up and speaking in front of groups. And kids were easier to entertain than adult coworkers. I was glad I got to give back my time and effort to the organization that really helped me when I needed it.

But back to high school; or what was left of it. I graduated in 1985, ready to start a new life. This was the start of my independence, when I would really come into my own.

PART 3: FAR FROM HOME: ASD LIFE AS A YOUNG ADULT

5
WELL, *THAT* DIDN'T WORK OUT AS PLANNED

A couple things happened as I graduated high school and began thinking about my future as an adult. While I did graduate a little young at seventeen, by my late teens most of the awkwardness of adolescence was gone. And, I was finally out of the clique environment – no more looks and giggles, no more mocking and bullying. I was soon to be on my own.

During the year after high school, I worked at a local drug store. Sometimes, I'd deliver medications to the local nursing home, and often I'd work in the basement as a receiving clerk. It was during this year that a change occurred. On the surface, it wasn't a big deal, but inside, it was the beginning of a new me with new confidence. I got contact lenses.

Since I was in fourth grade, I had to wear glasses. And, when you have Asperger's, styles that appeal to you usually don't appeal to everyone else. Haircut, clothes, and even glasses can mark you as either a cool kid or a complete dork. I was definitely the latter. I had changed my hair style since elementary school from straight bangs to parted in the middle and feathered back – the classic eighties look. Now I was no longer a four-eyes. Well, I was, but they were just really small and really close to my eyes, so you couldn't tell.

I also took a few basic college classes – an Intro to Psychology course, along with another one or two general ed courses that I could transfer into the four-year college of my choice. Getting out of the socio-emotional pit of high school opened me up in a new way. I was more confident around others. I was still awkward and shy around girls, but that was getting better slowly.

I really did have a great deal of empathy when I was a kid, and I enjoyed listening to others and helping them with their problems. It was natural, I guess, having gone through so much turmoil myself. It felt good to be able to help others. So, I wanted to be a counselor. Not just a counselor; a psychologist. I was heavily influenced by The Bob Newhart show. I had this romantic notion of being just like Bob in his office, having witty conversations with his patients and staff. That show, coupled with an Intro to Psych class I took during my senior year, and just like that, my mind was made up.

With a slightly better than dismal graduating GPA (I think it was just over a 2.0; yikes), one of the schools that would accept me AND had a good psych program was Western Michigan University. And so, in the fall of 1986, I packed up my 1977 Cutlass Supreme and, after saying goodbye to my mom and dad, I moved down to Kalamazoo and into full-time college life at WMU.

This was not the best idea for me, and I see now why many kids should not go straight off to college. The complete, unbridled freedom that is offered by moving away from home and into a dormitory is a gigantic temptation that can prove to be too much for many naïve teens. I even had a handicap going in. Based on a personality assessment, the university deemed me worthy of a single-occupancy room in an upper classmen's hall. Here's where my ASD-driven anti-social tendencies paid off.

It was a social experiment to see if "more mature" underclassmen could cohabitate with their elder peers, and I was one of the first. I was the lone freshman in a four-story dorm of juniors and seniors, mostly all either engineering or psychology majors. Granted, it was probably a better choice than living down in the zoo of freshman dorms, where there were roommates, loud music, and parties all the time.

I didn't represent very well. When you're already socially and emotionally mis-developed, having the kind of freedom that a large state university campus offers was not the best setting for me. I had my bike and my car, and I traveled all over campus and Kalamazoo. It was such an overwhelming explosion of new stimuli that I didn't know how to handle it. I stayed up late, and slept in, partying and skipping certain classes far more than I should have. I still wasn't good at math, so my entry-level college algebra course went horribly.

To make matters worse, the psychology program, touted as being led by a nationally renowned leader in the field, was not at all what I'd expected. I walked into my first psych courses, fully expecting to learn about people's behaviors and emotions; how their backgrounds and family life played into it, and some romantic fluff in the middle that would show me without question why people felt or acted certain ways, and how I would be able to help them.

It wasn't like that at all. It was purely behavioral psychology. Think of Pavlov and his dogs. Behavioral psych is a philosophy that people are prone to certain behaviors based solely on their surrounding environment. Certain outside stimuli will cause people to act a certain way.

To a behaviorist, there is no individual personality influence; they believe they can get a person, if they start that person young enough, to act however they choose. One of my first labs involved working with rats, and training them in mazes. I saw other rats in cages with electrodes going into the tops of their heads, connected to their brains. Signals pulsed through this wire or that would make them behave one way or the other.

This was not Bob Newhart, and this was not the romantic notion of psychology that I'd got from my couple of intro-level classes I had taken back home. The problem with this was, if I was a neurotypical young person devoted to learning psychology, I probably could've seen past these differences in program approach, even realizing I was in the real thick of it, that this is going to be the best. But I had a preconceived notion of what psychology was supposed to be about, and this program did not match that. Therefore, according to my neurodivergent way of thinking, the program was invalid, and I had to find another field of study.

Early in my first year of full-time college, I was faced with some real challenges, academic and otherwise. My mom called me one day to tell me that my dad had been let go from his job. He was not quite sixty years old at the time, and they had cut him loose *that* close to retirement. I was shocked and dismayed, ready to pack up and move back home to work to help support my family. But my mom assured me that wasn't necessary. After all, I was pretty much financially handling college on my own anyway, with what little I had in the bank coupled with a good chunk of Pell grant and student loans.

What she didn't know was that this news came during the time of the crisis I faced with my chosen field of study. I also hadn't been doing well in most of my classes. My grades suffered in my psych courses because I was disillusioned and wanted out of the program. Also, I was terrible at math, and I'd been skipping French class. My overall GPA was somewhere just north of 1.0. At least I'd succeeded at something: I bombed out of my first year of college.

My advisor recommended I take a semester or two the following year at a community college to bring my grade point up, and I could re-enroll at that time. I'd already switched my major to English with a computer science minor. I was reaching for something comfortable, and maybe, somewhere in the back of my head, I wanted to be a teacher. This does come heavily into play, albeit later on. For now, though, I had to settle for bombing out of Western and going to live with a friend in an apartment behind the football stadium.

With me, a nineteen-year-old small-town kid, rooming with my friend Mike, a mid-twenties Marine veteran, we couldn't have been more opposite. Mike was a big guy, as in, he'd gotten fairly overweight since leaving the Corps. And he had a stronger personality than I did. I was still a quiet, unassuming young guy who was still reveling in living in a big city on my own. Mike set up a neat arrangement – for himself. He'd do the cooking, and I'd do the cleaning. Yeah, great, for the first week. Otherwise, it was a cool place to live. I had a big bedroom upstairs, with the whole second floor all to myself. Mike was downstairs on the main floor. The apartment was the back part of a house, and two girls rented the front half.

Life quickly moved on. Within a couple of weeks of moving into the new apartment, I had enrolled in the local community college, three courses, and had already bought my books. Mike already had a job working second shift at a gas station out near the freeway. They needed a third shift clerk, so I was hired. I trained with Mike and one of the managers for three days and then on a Friday, I took my first shift on my own. I started at 11:00 pm and would work until 7:00 am, when the manager came in.

This would be my first – and last – night on the job. And in Kalamazoo.

For a Friday night, I don't remember it being that busy. I had some music playing on a big boombox, and I just sat at the counter and waited for customers to come in. This was the mid-80s, and believe it or not, gas stations still offered full service. I kept about $75 in cash in my shirt pocket, and if someone pulled up to the full-serve pump, I'd go out and pump their gas, and complete the transaction – in cash. Credit cards were not nearly as commonplace, either.

Shortly after midnight it had died right down. Nobody was coming in. It was quiet...almost *too* quiet. Then, at about 1:00 am, an older guy walked in. I forget who said, "How ya doin'?" first, because he immediately walked right behind the counter, put a knife to my side, and said, "You know what I want." I couldn't believe it. Even though I'd been shaken down by a punk thug waving a knife around in middle school for a box of tic tacs he heard rattling in my pocket ("Drugs!"), I'd never actually been robbed at knifepoint like this. At least I knew the knucklehead who caught me behind the public library that day – the same punk who'd given me a red belly on my first day of seventh grade.

This was a stranger, quite a bit older. He had gray in his hair, and he wasn't waving his knife around – he had the point to my gut. I didn't know if he was going to thank me or stick me. I opened the drawer and handed him the cash – about $200. As I stood there in shock, he walked back around the counter and on his way out, he said, "Now, don't call the cops or nothin'."

I just sat on the stool, stunned and immobile. Shock and disbelief were my reality at that moment. I saw nothing, heard nothing for several minutes. That is, until a car pulled up out front and a young guy got out of the car and came in, asking directions to some place. I watched him the whole time. I watched his car pull up, him get out and say something to the girl in the passenger seat, push the glass door open and walk up to the counter, saying he'd got turned around and was looking for such-and-such street. But he didn't even really register to me. I just looked at him and said, "man, I can't think right now, sorry, I just got robbed."

How he acted next was ironic. He freaked out – for me, I guess – and said, "Oh, s**t! Yeah, never mind! You should call the police!" And out the door he ran. It was funny, really. Here I was, sitting in the aftermath of an armed robbery, calm and cool though it may have been, the guy long gone, and this poor guy about wets himself being witness to...me, after the fact? I get it. Defense mechanisms kick in – who knows in those cases, maybe someone is still lurking nearby, maybe to do some follow up work. At any rate, the poor dude bolted and was gone.

That snapped me out of it. He was right, what was that guy going to do? Come back with the cops there? "I told you not to call them, man!" So, I dialed 911 and reported an armed robbery at the Amoco station on University Drive by the U.S. 131 interchange. Within a few minutes the police arrived. One officer came in to talk to me, while another surveyed the property inside and out. He interviewed me for the details of the perp, exactly what was said, and which way he went when he left. They brought a K-9 unit in to try and sniff him out, but they lost his scent not far from the station.

By this time, I was over being scared, and I was mad. How could some gray-haired old dude come in and rob me like that? I had called the manager right after talking to the police and told him that I still had the $75 in my pocket, and I'd stay open until he got there in the morning. As the police were getting ready to leave, the officer I had spoken with gave me a piece of advice. To this day, I remember it, because his advice saved my life. He told me to close and lock the door, and only open it for people that I knew were paying customers. Good idea! I thanked him, and they left. I should note that the only real security measure the station had for its employees was a back room with a big steel door that you could bolt shut from the inside.

What happened next was like something out of a movie. As I watched their taillights head across the lot toward the road, I got up and went around the counter, and locked the glass front door. I no sooner had got back around the counter and sat down, when two guys in white hoodies came running around the front of the building.

The guy in front had a long gun in his hands, and they tried to bust their way into the store. The first guy rammed his shoulder into the door, bounced off, and when they realized they'd been foiled, they took off. At least I'm assuming they did. I'm not sure, because I had dropped like a rock to the floor, behind the counter. I reached up blindly and grabbed the phone and re-dialed 911 to report a second hit on the station.

With me cowering in abject fear behind the counter, and the door locked, I waited in petrified silence for the police to arrive. I'm quite sure I was visibly shaking. After several long minutes, I thought I heard people outside, but I was too scared to get up and look. I thought the thugs were still out there, waiting for me to show my face so they could blow it off.

There was a sudden "THUMP-THUMP-THUMP!" on the window right above my head. I gasped a breath in, sure it was them, trying to break in the window, so for a minute I cowered even further down. Then something made me look up, and it was the police. The same officer I'd spoken to before, in fact. They couldn't get in because the door was locked, and there weren't cell phones yet so he couldn't call me to let me know he was out there.

I got up and opened the door for them. Once again, he took my report, and tried to assure me that he didn't think this crazy second time-around was related to the first incident. But I knew better. The first guy told me not to call the cops, but I called them anyway, and they tried to sniff him out. The other two guys had come to make me pay.

By then, I was done. It was after 3 am by that point, and I was too scared and exhausted to stay open. I'm not sure either the manager or the police would've let me, anyway. So, I called the manager back, told him what happened, and that I'd lock up and be back at 7 am to open it up for him.

I had the police escort me back to the apartment. I went inside, locked all the doors, went to my roommate's bedroom. He was out of town, home in Grand Rapids for the weekend. I got his 20-gauge shotgun out of his closet. I loaded it and didn't go anywhere in the apartment without it. Mind you, I was smoking at this time of my life – another great habit I picked up in my first year of freedom. I chain-smoked two and a half packs of cigarettes in about two or three hours. I was just a bit on edge.

That settled it. I'd had enough of this crazy town. I wouldn't be going back to Western any time soon, and I really didn't know what I wanted to do when I got there anyway. So that day, Saturday, I packed most of my stuff in my suitcase and headed home to Cadillac.

It was double-settled about as soon as I got home that I wouldn't be returning to Kalamazoo, ever. My mom wouldn't have it. I couldn't really blame her, or find a good reason to go back; it was good to be home. So, I called my roommate on Sunday when he was back at the house. I told him I couldn't live down there, and I sure couldn't go back to work at that gas station. I was going to tell the manager that I quit on Monday.

At first, he mocked me, telling me that when he was still in the service, he got jumped by five guys one night after leaving a bar, and beat them all up. Well, that's great – you're a twenty-seven-year-old ex-marine, I'm a nineteen-year-old small-town kid. He tried to talk me into coming back down in a week. I told him I'd come down during the next week to get the rest of my stuff.

A couple of days later, his tone had changed dramatically. He called me late on Monday night, at about 10:30. When I picked up, the first words out of his mouth were, "You were right!" He was working his second shift that night and was going to have to lock up at 11:00, since I wasn't there to work the midnight shift. He told me how at about 8:00, a car pulled in with two shady looking characters in it. They parked in the lot off to one side, and just sat there watching the station. One of them came in after a while for a soda and some cigarettes.

He started watching them, clearly visible in the window, and after they saw him watching for a bit, they left. But, he said, they came back a little while later with another guy in the car, and just sat and stared at the building. This time, they weren't worried about him watching them. By now it was about 9:30 at night. Mike was supposed to start wrapping things up about 10:15 to close for the night.

He picked up the phone and set it on the counter, right in the window where they could see it, and called the police. He told them this was the same station that was hit twice on Friday night, and now he had three guys in the parking lot scoping the place out. That did it. The thugs saw him talking to the cops, and they left. The police showed up a few minutes later, and Mike closed up early, and had them escort him back to the apartment.

So, the fear was real. I actually had a very short-term bout of PTSD from the experience. I remember sitting upstairs in my room during that first week back home, looking out the window, and feeling a sudden dread hit me: what if they knew where I lived? What if I'd crossed some gang, and they ALWAYS tied up their loose ends? It was not unreasonable to me, in that moment, to think that they'd drive 150 miles north to end the pain in their rear end, who almost got one of them caught. For all I knew, the police were onto them now, and those thugs were hating me with all their might.

This was quite a lot of extreme stimulation for one young neurodivergent brain. I kind of settled in back home and tried to figure out what to do next with my life. For once, I enjoyed the slow, dull pace of a small town. I started by getting a job back at the drug store I'd worked at in high school. My mom knew the pharmacist and owner, and she called in a favor for me.

When I worked there in high school and just after, I did deliveries to the local nursing home and worked in the basement doing receiving. But now, he really didn't have much for me to do, so he put me to work upstairs, in what was essentially the attic of the building. He had me cleaning out a bunch of old junk that had been stored up there over the years. It was busy work, we both knew it, and I was in a bit of a funk.

In my mind, I'd tried, and failed, at college life. Now I was a flunky stuck back at home with no real prospects for the future. I got lazy at work, and I think this was due to being mildly depressed about my situation. This didn't sit well with the boss, who repeatedly came upstairs and found me lazing about. He finally got upset and told me he was trying to do right by my mom and help me out, but it just wasn't working out.

I bounced around a few different minimum wage jobs. I was drinking and partying. I had a couple of short-term girlfriends. I was basically living it up, living life and having fun. My friend Todd came back from the army, and we hung out a lot. It was good times, a catharsis to get rid of my pent-up energy and craziness, and to get over what life had thrown at me so far. After a year or so of this, my dad made a suggestion that would end up setting me on a new course for the rest of my life.

6
COMING OF AGE

In early 1988, I was twenty years old and still working a minimum wage job, trying to figure out life. One thing I'd been doing a lot at this point was drawing – something I'd done since I was little.

I was generally more comfortable doing more "technical" drawing, where I used a ruler, and made exact, straight-line types of drawings. It was basically impromptu drafting. They were usually just geometric shapes. I could do the freehand sketching, but it took longer and I wasn't as comfortable without a ruler or straightedge in my hand. One day I was sitting at our dining room table at home, doing one of my "technical" doodles, when my dad offered a suggestion.

When he got fired from his job as the plant engineer at a local manufacturing company, he took some time off to de-stress. He then found what turned out to be the perfect role for him – working as a parapro at the Career Tech Center helping to teach high school kids in the CAD & Drafting program. Since my dad had just turned sixty, he wasn't very familiar with computers, so he mainly taught the old-school board drafting. The basis for all drafting, even Computer Aided Drafting (CAD) starts with the trigonometric and geometric basics learned on the drawing board.

So, I went back to school with my dad as one of my teachers. Oddly, this wasn't awkward for me at all. And, as it turned out…I loved drafting, and CAD. I took to it like a fish in water. I had found my thing. That two-year technical course was life-changing for me. I loved it; it gave me purpose.

Geometry and right-angle trigonometry were taught in tandem during the board drafting part of the class. And, it just so happened that…the trig clicked in my mind right away. I *could* learn math! I *did* learn math, and liked it. This was, pardon the cliche, a game-changer for me. It's like having a jigsaw puzzle half complete, and you're just stuck. Then, out of the corner of your eye, you spot the ONE piece. The piece that you've not only been looking for, but helps link the entire puzzle together.

This was a huge moment. The biggest light bulb went off. I had an epiphany – I knew I had conquered math. Not just the trig, but all of it. You know the saying that when you get something, it finally clicks? That was what it was like, in a literal sense. My brain clicked into a different gear when it got the trig. I can't remember anything like it before. In that moment I knew that what my dad had told me all my life was true: you can do anything if you put your mind to it and work at it. It wouldn't be long before this revelation would start shaping my life for the better beyond the CAD classroom.

I went from the drawing board to the CAD station. I loved that, too. I took to it like a duck to water. It was a beautiful blending of my two favorite pastimes – straight-line drawing, like I used to do with rulers and templates, and the user-friendly computer interface gave CAD a video game-esque appeal. I could sit for hours and "doodle" technical drawings.

My own personal crowning project was a perfect blending of two of my favorite things: CAD and railroading. I had drawn, in exacting detail, a diesel locomotive. The couplers had air hoses, the side panels had vents, the windows had windshield wipers. It was a labor of love, and by definition a work of art. I don't have it any more, it was long ago lost at my parents' house. The electronic data file had been stored on a 3 ½" floppy disk. Heh, good luck getting it off of *that*.

I graduated the two-year CAD & Drafting program at the top of my class – an academic first. It seemed I was onto something. While I didn't fully realize it then, my specialty, my keen interest would turn out to be technical and mechanical. I had always wanted to be more of an artist, the creative type; an author, a great writer of novels. But, we do the best with what we're given. And at that time, my mathematical and technical abilities were really shining through.

My first technical job was a temporary contract position that my dad hooked me up with. He knew a guy who was a distributor of machined parts, fasteners and such. He was looking for someone to do some technical drawings for him, 2D and isometric component "sketches" for a catalog he was putting together. He asked what my price was. This was a milestone; my first real negotiation for the use of my technical skills. I offered $7.00 per hour, and he accepted.

This was the late 1980s, and minimum wage was about $3.75 per hour. When you compare that to today, where $10.00 to $15.00 is the going starting rate most places, then I was effectively earning, by today's standards, between $20.00 and $25.00 an hour as a pure newbie, a 100% rookie with zero experience. Ironically though, my dad chided me for offering such a low starting wage and told me to respect my own ability and charge for it. Truthfully, I was just happy for the opportunity, and to be making some money on the side.

As far as my home life, it was about this time that my best friend from high school and I decided to rent a place together, and so it was time to move out of Mom and Dad's house. As much as they loved me, I think they were ready for my independence as much as I was. That year or two after Kalamazoo left me coming home quite late some nights, and not always in the best shape. It was time for me to go do my thing somewhere else. So, Denny and I rented a small, shabby bungalow on the other side of Lake Cadillac, and my independence began in earnest. From this point on, there was no looking back.

At this point in my life, I can't say that my ASD was really affecting me all that much. I had successfully completed a technical training course, I had landed my first real job using the skills that I loved, and I was living on my own again, in my early twenties. Life was great and only getting better.

And then, my first REAL job came to be…at a company that would have a significant impact on my life, in many ways. A small but spirited electronics manufacturing outfit in Reed City, Michigan was looking for a CAD detailer to revise their engineering drawings. They used the same CAD system that I'd learned on and was an expert with. I was a shoo-in. I applied, got an interview right away and was hired.

I loved my work; it was everything a high-functioning Aspie of my persuasion could ask for: A computer system that let you create, generate drawings of a very technical, precise nature. My title was "CAD Detailer", so details were thus important, and this was a slam-dunk for my detail-oriented ASD brain. I did have to interact with others, like my coworkers and my boss. But for the most part, I sat by myself in front of my screen and drew. Life was good. I was out of my parents' house and rooming with my best friend from high school, I had my first real job that I enjoyed greatly.

I would also meet the love of my life. I didn't know it right away when it happened, but it happened nonetheless.

I went through a very significant, conscious change during this time. I rebranded myself. For most of my life, I had been this awkward, geeky kid who didn't fit in. I think even my family, as much as family members care for each other, didn't expect me to amount to much. After a couple of years outside of high school, having gone through some trials and come through mostly unscathed, it was time to start doing what others thought I'd never do.

It was a very profound, conscious moment of deciding to take action on a new course for life. It was a "do or die" moment where I was at a figurative fork in the road. I could continue down the same road I'd always been on, not expecting much and not getting much from life. Or, I could "take the road less traveled," and that's exactly what I did.

I had done some working out with a friend down the hall from me at Western. And, after a year or so back home, a friend I met while working at one of my short-term jobs got me to start going to a local health club regularly. It felt good to get in shape. It was at this point that I decided fitness was going to be front and center in my life. This same friend who I had been going to the health club with was also into "breaking his chains" and wanted to try new things. We were both terribly afraid of heights, so when we weren't pumping iron, we climbed iron towers.

There was a 200-foot-tall radio tower on the southern outskirts of Cadillac. Back in those days, pieces of infrastructure such as giant towers weren't very secured, so we were able to easily walk up to the base of it. Running up the middle to the top was an iron-rung ladder, allowing a worker access for repair of the dishes near the top, or to replace the red blinking light at the very top.

So, Jay and I, looking to slay one of the giants in our lives, started climbing the ladder in order to overcome our acrophobia. The first couple of times, neither one of us could get more than six to eight feet off the ground. But we kept at it, a few nights a week, usually more than one try per night. And we did it. Eventually, we both scaled the entire height, slapped the thick red glass lens of the blinking light at the top, and thus we had mastered our fear. Nothing could stop us now.

The changes kept coming. I was getting in shape, and I'd conquered a lifelong fear of heights (and that wasn't done *yet*). One thing about my life at that point was that girlfriends were few and far between, and my relationships didn't last long. The longest I'd dated anyone was three months. Even with all this exciting new stuff happening in my life, I didn't have a special someone. But honestly, at that time, I didn't miss it.

Instead, I moved out of Cadillac altogether and down to Big Rapids. I was now closer to work, and just a block away from Ferris State University. I was enjoying life and moving forward with a career, and soon-to-be new college experience. Again, at my dad's suggestion, I looked into the Engineering programs Ferris offered.

There was something I never thought I'd be considering: a degree in an engineering discipline. Think of the math involved! Truth be told, in high school I wasn't that great at science, either. Chemistry and physics went way over my head, being formula-based sciences. Physics is very algebra-themed. If you don't have math-friendly mind, it's not going to pick up on those two subjects very well.

But that was different now; the epiphany from my drafting days was coming to fruition, and so began my endeavor toward another college degree. I took, a little at a time, some of the beginning courses toward an Associates in Applied Science for Mechanical Engineering Technology.

Thankfully, some of the basic entry courses from Western transferred, but I did start at FSU during an accelerated summer term with a course called Statics and Strengths of Materials. And, wouldn't you know it…physics was a prerequisite for this class.

But, my academic advisor (who was also the professor for the class) felt that I could handle it and was willing to wave the prereq requirement. And so, with what would become the mantra of my life, I jumped in and just did it. In the summer of 1991, I signed up for an accelerated physics-based engineering course, without having ever taken college-level physics.

The house I moved into was a blast. One of the guys I worked with lived there, with five other guys, and they were looking for one more roommate. It was great because all the other guys, except for Regan, the guy I worked with, were all either Ferris football players or weightlifters.

By then I'd put on some size and strength, had been running, had mostly kicked the smoking habit, and was in pretty good shape, so I fit right in. Regan, on the other hand, was a skinny, smart-mouthed partier who liked to smoke, drink and hit on girls. One of the more hilarious roommates was Jeff; a big offensive lineman for the Bulldog football team. Jeff could bench 400 pounds. A lot of people would've taken him for just another meathead; but to me, he was personable, funny, and liked to joke around.

Regan made the mistake of mouthing off to Jeff one day, while the two of them were home alone. Jeff picked Regan up with one hand and threw him across the living room. Then the best part happened – you really can't make this up. Regan went to a party that weekend and started talking to a girl. He was telling her what a jerk his roommate Jeff was, although I'm sure he used more colorful language. The girl turned out to be Jeff's girlfriend. Ah, the irony.

We hardly saw Regan for two weeks. In the evening, while a bunch of us would be sitting in the living room watching TV, Regan would come in the front door, poke his head around the corner, see Jeff sitting there, and in a flash, he was up the stairs to his room. He'd get up and go to work the next day, and repeat.

What a weird but wonderful time. During my entire childhood, right through high school, I was a freak, a spaz, an awkward geek that wasn't good at anything athletic. This isn't a surprise to me now. It turns out people with ASD are usually pretty uncoordinated. So, sports and us don't usually get along.

I had played little league T-ball and baseball in early elementary. When we started using pitchers, I got hit by the ball once, right in the side of the head. I was wearing a helmet, but it still hurt. From that day forward I was deathly afraid to go to bat. When I was in the outfield, I was bored, and missed most of the balls that were hit in my direction. I tried baseball one more time in high school, but wasn't much better. I had gone to Tae Kwon Do for a year or so in middle school, but never got past a yellow belt. As far as weightlifting, other than occasionally using the cheap old K-Mart set of weights my dad had in the garage, I never did much of that either.

The jocks in school never really picked on me, but they didn't buddy up to me either. They just kind of ignored me or maybe chuckled at me from the side. I sure wasn't part of their group. And now, here I was, in a house full of college football players and weightlifters, and I was one of the guys. It was almost surreal. Someone else was the outcast instead of me. And really, Regan didn't have to be the outcast if he didn't want to, but he couldn't help running his mouth. His buddy from high school back home was one of the football players, so that's how he got into the house. Six big, burly guys, and skinny little smart-aleck Regan. It was fun, and I'd do it all over again.

I had found empathy along the way of growing up and getting bigger. An obvious reason I started working out in the first place was to build confidence. I didn't want to be the skinny geek who got picked on anymore. As I grew and experienced other people and places, I realized I needed to look out for those who were less fortunate than me, not pick on them in turn.

My experience with girls changed in short order, and in a way that took me completely by surprise. There was definitely something about that place and time in my life that was fundamentally life changing. It took me to a whole other level.

One Saturday in early August of 1991, the VP of the company was having a party at his house. I was in the front office a few days before the party, and this girl who'd moved back to town recently was working in the front office. Her name was Tammy. She was pretty cute, but after the less than stellar luck I'd had with girlfriends, I mostly kept to myself. Anyway, Tammy asked me if I was planning to go to the party. I said I hadn't really thought about it, but I guess so. She was hoping I'd go. I said sure, but after that I didn't think too much else of it.

But first, on that same Saturday, Jay and I had one more major chain to break to prove once and for all we'd beaten our fear of heights. Early in the day, we went to a little airport in a little town about forty miles southwest of Big Rapids to take our first skydiving lesson and complete a 4,000-foot static line jump.

I had never flown before, and I was going to strap on a parachute and throw myself out of an airplane thousands of feet in the air. That's where my head was at that time. I thought it might be a good idea to see what flying was like first. One of the engineers that worked at Nartron was a guy named Mark who happened to have his pilot's license. He also happened to have his own Cessna. He also happened to live in the Detroit area and flew to work each week, landing at the old airstrip and hangar that was part of Nartron's property. It was also where the Advanced Product Design building was located, where we all worked.

I told Mark my plan and asked him if he'd take me up so I at least knew what it was like to fly before the big day. He thought I was crazy for wanting to jump out of a plane, but he was more than happy to oblige. He was heading up to the Wexford County airport in Cadillac to fuel up for the weekend. To my surprise, he actually let me handle part of the takeoff.

Flying in a little Cessna four-seat propeller plane wasn't that different from riding in a car, once you leveled off. It was really cool, being up in the clouds, more than 200 feet in the air for the first time. I was glad I did it.

The following weekend was our date with destiny. Jay and I drove like maniacs to the little airport in Grant, Michigan. I was driving and at one point we were doing at least 70 in a 55-mph zone. We ended up getting pulled over by a sheriff's deputy. He walked up to the car and asked if I knew how fast I was going. We were so hyped that I just said yes, then I told him my speed at the time he clocked me, and apologized. We both told him we were on our way to our first skydiving session, and we were just so hyped that we lost track of our speed. He laughed. Apparently, that was one of the craziest things he'd heard. He let us go with just a warning.

When we got there, we were all ushered into this little single-wide trailer. The first half of the day was instruction. Three to four hours of video and live instruction on everything from our legal rights to the history of the airport to equipment maintenance, including how to pack your own chute, to making the jump itself. Hurling yourself out of a perfectly good airplane while thousands of feet in the air is serious business. There was, of course, training on how to pull your emergency chute if the main one failed to open. And how to get out of something called a "line twist". It was a lot of information to pack into our heads, and then we were sent off to the wild blue yonder for the ultimate final exam.

While we were donning our gear and get ready to load into the plane (which was *not* perfectly good, with duct tape on the engine cowling), I was a little nervous but tried not to show it. Jay was nervous and hyped, and loudly showing it. That was Jay. I'm an introvert, he's an extrovert – always animated, smiling, greeting with a loud voice. And getting hyped out of his pants in the same fashion.

We wore helmets with a one-way radio receivers mounted in them, goggles, altimeters strapped to our wrists, jumpsuits, and our packs with main and emergency chutes. A number of us, I think about four, plus the pilot and an instructor, all boarded the battered cargo bird that would take us to meet our fate. I was glad I had taken that first flight with Mark. Some of the guys had never been in a plane before, so they were clearly tightening up as we climbed to 4,000 feet.

They trained us so that when it was our turn, we'd be in position next to the door. The instructor would open the door, and we'd swing our legs out onto the step. We'd then grab ahold of the angled wing strut, and hand-crawl our way out onto the strut, our legs now dangling and flying behind us.

That was the scariest moment of my life. I was wishing for my mother and praying that I wouldn't die. We were going a little over 100 mph at 4,000 feet, and I was dangling from the wing of an airplane. Any comforting thought of the gear on my back and the failsafe tether that would pull open the chute was nowhere to be found. I wasn't thinking about anything except how terrified I was and when, oh when could I let go of this strut and have all this be over?

What I'm sure was seconds felt like long, drawn-out minutes. We were told to wait for a thumbs-up from the instructor before letting go. I was staring intently – and I'm sure a little wild-eyed –

at the window. The instructor was grinning from ear to ear, savoring my terror. He finally held a thumb up, and I let go. And then…everything was fine. In fact, it was wonderful.

The chute opened without issue, and in an instant, I was floating, gliding down, still a few thousand feet in the air. It was amazing. You could see so much, but everything was so small it was hard to take in the scale at first.

A partner instructor on the ground would radio instructions to us; pull the left cord and turn to the left, straighten out, pull both cords slightly and brake. He told us to keep an eye on our altimeter, and the ground. He talked us down, all the way to the target landing area, and I came in for an almost perfect two-point landing. I was so hyped I couldn't stand it. It was, and still is, one of the most amazing things I've done in my life. It was so amazing, in fact, that we went back two more times before the season ended.

During our second jump, there was a family there – a dad and his two sons, Brian and Dan. They were going up separately in the two flights ahead of Jay and me. The dad and Brian went first. The ground instructor got the brothers' names mixed up on the sheet, and after Brian jumped out, the instructor started calling directions to Dan. Brian realized what had happened, so he followed the commands and came in for a safe landing. Dan wasn't so lucky. He must've thought Brian was still in the air or something. When the ground instructor started calling Dan "Brian", Dan didn't react…at all. He just hung there in the air. Because he wasn't turning or braking, he floated off and landed in a cornfield.

He was a little banged up but mostly unharmed. The dad was really angry and wanted his money back for their jumps. Skydiving is not cheap, and even though the static line method is less expensive than the 10,000-foot freefall, it was still $180 per person. And that was in the early 1990s. It's probably more now.

On my third and what would be my final jump, I had an equipment malfunction. Remember I said they trained us how to deal with line twists? That's what I got, and it was a doozy. If this happens, they told us, DON'T PANIC. Reach up, grab the straps that extend from your pack, and start pulling them apart and kicking your feet. This causes you to rotate in the air, and it unwinds the lines. Something didn't feel quite right when the tether pulled my chute. I looked up and saw a flailing ball of fabric that was the chute, and the twisted lines.

Amazingly, I didn't panic. In my head, I thought, "I have no choice here. If I want to get out of this alive, I have to do this."

I'm sure my ground instructor was giving me directions, but I don't remember hearing anything. All I remember is remaining very calm, and very deliberately looking up, assessing the problem, and moving into action. It was textbook: I reached up, grabbed the lines, noticed which direction they were twisted, started kicking in the other direction. Within seconds they unwound enough for the chute to inflate. I glided down and made a slightly rough and abrupt landing, but I was otherwise unscathed.

I've since watched videos online of skydivers dealing with line twists. With their GoPros on their helmets, they seem to start out calm enough, but I've heard enough mumbling and cursing to know that they're not entirely calm as they try to unravel their lines. In each of these, they had mild twists – their chutes were mostly inflated, but they had no control. How and why I remained so calm in my situation, I can't explain. I'm sure part of it was "ignorance is bliss". When something like that's never happened to you before, you don't realize how serious it is.

Another part of my "calm amidst the storm" was my ASD brain kicking in. Socially I'm more of an emotional thinker than logical. But when a problem arises, the logic and single-minded focus kick in. I block out everything else except the situation in front of me, and what I need to do to solve it. I saved my dad from choking once by giving him the Heimlich maneuver. That was at a birthday party for my uncle, and there were a lot of people there.

Everyone just sat there, stunned, looking around and shouting for help. I did the same thing for my father-in-law years ago. In each of these situations, there was really no panic. I think a big part of it is just instinctual. I automatically think, "If I don't do something, I (or this other person) may die", and in the same instant I'm taking action. I don't know how else to explain it.

After the very first jump, Jay and I were higher than kites, no pun intended. After I dropped him off at his car in Reed City, I raced back to my house in Big Rapids. I had planned on going up to Cadillac to spend the second half of the weekend up there, and to tell my family and friends about this most incredible experience.

I had completely forgotten about the company party, and was ready to throw a few clothes in a bag and head north when I saw the casserole I'd made for the party in the refrigerator. "Ah, that's right! The party. Well, I can stop by for a while and then head up to Cadillac later at night, I thought to myself. Mark was going to be there, and he was very curious to know what it was like to jump out of a perfectly good airplane. So, I figured I'd stop by for a while, talk to a few people, and head home afterwards.

While I did talk to a few people, mainly Mark and the people at his table about the crazy, exhilarating experience of gliding from 4,000 feet to the ground, I also met up with Tammy. As preoccupied with the crazy weekend I'd had so far, and as much as I was enjoying life and not really looking for anyone special at that moment, it was clear very quickly that we both liked each other very much. We hit it off right away, spent a lot of the weekend together talking and getting to know each other.

I was always emotionally awkward around girls, even when we were dating. That was how my neurodivergent brain worked. Social awkwardness, along with roller-coaster emotions, did not make me a great mate for long. But with Tammy, it was different. That awkwardness wasn't there. I was taking it slow and controlled for once in my life. I really believe this was one of the first and main sign from God that we were meant to be. He helped reign in my usual ASD quirks.

And so began another chapter of my new life: my life with a girl, the girl who would become the love of my life and my wife of twenty-eight years. We're still married, in fact. I mentioned before that this was how my feelings worked – when I was in, I was all in. I wasn't even looking to meet anyone at that time in my life. But there was a connection, for sure. We were just what the other needed.

PART 4: ASD LIFE AS A HUSBAND AND A FATHER

7
THINGS GET A LITTLE STRANGE

Just as life was going well, it decided to throw me a curve ball.

They say God has a weird sense of humor; I think God does what He does in love and good humor, but not to prank us. Trials and even failures are where we learn and grow best.

It was August 3rd of 1991 when Tammy and I met. She was just starting college at Ferris to get an Associate's degree in Child Development. She wanted to be a pre-school teacher. I continued to live in the pseudo-frat house until fall. By then the lease was up, and everyone was going their own way. I needed a new place to live.

Robert, a newer engineer at Nartron, had just bought a house in the nearby town of Evart, and he had an extra room he was willing to rent out. So, I moved from Big Rapids to Evart, from a houseful of crazy football players and weightlifters a block off of campus to a quiet, rural town with quiet, studious roommates. Robert was soft-spoken, a typical engineer. He moved his childhood friend John into the house also. John was a big guy, and more talkative than Robert, but still more reserved and intellectual than my former friends.

I got the bedroom in the back, right off the kitchen. Robert was lodged in the front of the house, across from the bathroom. And John was upstairs. A crazy weekend for these guys involved having Robert's brother come visit and the three of them would sit in the living room and play Dungeons and Dragons late into the night. Tammy and the boys were bunking with her parents, so she would come over and we'd hang out.

We continued dating, and I continued working as a CAD detailer at Nartron, and I successfully completed my first engineering course, double-paced and without the prerequisite. Life was good.

Nartron did business in a few different arenas. These included commercial, automotive, and military products. You'd think the diversity would help keep things busy, but in early 1992, the follow-through of the completion of the Gulf war from a year earlier caught up. When a military action is completed, the Pentagon always gathers in the civilian contracts it has active and weeds them out. Many will get shut down.

That happened to Nartron's business. With a good chunk of their sales suddenly shut off, a layoff followed, and I was one of the casualties. So was Robert, who had just bought his house a few months before, almost sight-unseen. Now he was forced to put it back up for sale and head back to Midland. By this time, about six months into our relationship, Tammy and I knew it was serious. Agreeing we were in for the long haul, we got an apartment together.

It wasn't easy, but it was fun and I had an instant start on my family. Tammy's ex-husband was mostly out of the picture at this time – he was still down south – and so I was raising the boys with her. By this time, Troy was five and Terry was almost two years old. It was actually a great time in our family relationship. I played video games with the boys and told them bedtime stories.

Our engagement was pretty pragmatic; as I said, we knew early on that this was it, we were together for the long haul. I proposed to her in late 1992, and we married a year later. I held different jobs around town to support us, at one point being night security for a local inn. Tammy did some part time daycare while she studied. Again, it was a bumpy start, but we were young, energetic and motivated. We loved each other and our fledgling family was taking off.

I was born and raised Catholic, but had fallen away from church when I was a teenager. Since Tammy and I were together, though, I had a renewed interest in growing my faith. We started attending church pretty regularly. But our joint faith journey took us to protestant denominations – mainly Baptist and Assembly of God. Good old churches that just preach the Word right out of the Bible, and encourage you to read along.

I had a strong interest in completing what I'd left off earlier in life. In line with my newfound interest in strengthening my faith walk with God, my sister and I both enrolled in confirmation classes at St. Paul's campus parish. Our family came for the ceremony where Becky and I were officially confirmed in the Catholic church. Ironic that it would be the last time that I ever attended a Catholic service, except for funerals.

On July 31, 1993, Tammy and I became Mr. and Mrs. Klubeck. We ended up getting married in a little white church in a small town outside of Reed City. We honeymooned at Niagara Falls, on the U.S. side, while my sister stayed with the boys in our apartment. We returned after a week's vacation, and now officially the Klubeck family, our domestic life was finally settled.

I was twenty-five when I got married, and things were mostly good, ASD-wise. We had lived together for a couple of years as a makeshift mini-family, and everything had gone well. My Asperger's traits seemed all but nonexistent. Right after we got married, I think the reality of the situation overwhelmed me briefly. I remember having one or two big arguments with Tammy that blew up and then blew out as quickly as they'd come. Other than that, I had no real stressors, no sensory overloads at that time. I was hanging out with friends, working, and living with my new family.

There was just one more step that needed to be taken – I was going to adopt the boys. Tammy had been talking to her ex, and he agreed that the best situation form them was for him to sign off his parental rights and allow me to adopt them. His life was, um, a bit complicated, and he wasn't able to visit with them more than a couple of times a year. By allowing me to adopt them, the complete family bond created a security that gave the boys a stability beyond being "step kids". I considered them to be my own children, and loved and raised them as such. The adoption process didn't happen immediately, but a couple of years into our marriage when Terry was four, and Troy was seven years old.

When Troy was about seven, he really wanted to play football. Tammy was worried about concussions and tried to think of other sports that were less hazardous to his health. So, we came up with the bright idea of…hockey. At first, Troy was a little reluctant, but when he watched some Red Wings games and he saw the hits that Vladimir Konstantinov (the Vladinator, Vlad the Impaler) was throwing at his opponents, he realized he didn't need to play football to hit people. Here was a sport he could get into – razor sharp blades on his feet, a big stick in his hands, and flying up the ice faster than he could run. He was sold.

And so was I, not long after. We started Troy in skating lessons with a figure skating coach. This really is the most important part of the sport. You can pick up the other skills along the way, but you need to have good skates and be a strong skater. This was skating for hockey, though, so the kids all wore their full gear while practicing. We started going to Ferris State hockey games. It was a blast. Between watching Troy at practice and our division 1 Bulldog team playing against the likes of MSU and Michigan, I was hooked. I had to learn how to skate. I wanted to play.

Remember when I said that people with ASD aren't usually the most coordinated? Well, that applied me and hockey. Not to mention, I was teaching myself…as an adult. A far cry from taking lessons and learning as a young child. I taught myself to skate for a year before going all in, buying all the gear, and signing up for a men's league. When I stepped on the ice for the first time in a league game, I realized how far I had yet to go. By the second period I was so exhausted that when I went to line up for a face-off, I was on the other side of the circle, with the other team. I didn't even realize where I was.

It got better, though. We both did. Troy became an amazing defenseman. He was a complete blast to watch. When Troy was coming up in the early 2000s, youth hockey let the kids start checking, or hitting at the Peewee level. This starts at age eleven. That's what he'd been waiting for. It didn't take him long to be a terror on the ice. When the other team would bring the puck out of their zone, Troy would skate backwards, keeping the puck carrier in his sights. He'd slow and close the gap a little, always watching. The minute the kid took his eyes off Troy and looked down at the puck, he was over. Troy would brake, brace and just level the kid.

It sounds brutal, but I remember only a very few times when anyone got really hurt from a big check. Troy got his wrist sprained getting knocked into the boards when he was in high school, but other than that, he never got seriously injured. No concussions, thank goodness. Beyond knocking the stuffing out of opponents, he was a really solid skater and could handle the puck pretty well. He almost made it on a junior team, but the competition was fierce by the time they reached that level.

As far as my hockey career, I learned to be a solid skater. I never did have the dexterity to be a great puck handler, so I also specialized in defense during the first several years of playing. I found that I liked skating backwards better than trying to carry the puck through opposing players, which I couldn't. Thanks, Asperger's. I could carry the puck well enough if no one was on me. But the minute someone was, I was pressured and I'd panic. I couldn't carry it if it had handles. I would inevitably cough it up and the other team would recover it.

But, like Troy, I found defense to be rather satisfying. Most men's leagues don't allow blatant checking, but you can "bump and rub", make incidental contact if you're going for the puck. I made a specialty out of incidentally knocking opponents on their cans. I got my share of whistles and time in the penalty box, but it was fun. I was literally a freight train the first twelve to fifteen years of playing hockey. My size and strength, lack of coordination, and penchant for hitting things earned me that nickname: Freight Train.

A new guy had joined our 40 and over league several years ago. He was a hotshot, had played as a kid through high school, and was set to play for Michigan State but got hurt and had to quit. But when he healed, he obviously kept playing in other leagues because he was inarguably the best player at the time he joined with us.

He was good, and big, and he knew it. A cocky alpha male, he'd come flying into the zone at top speed, and when he was well inside the blue line wind up and he'd let off a 100-mph slap shot. He was aggressive and he'd crowd opposing players, forcing them into the boards and off the puck.

One time he fired a slapshot that hit our goalie's helmet so hard that it knocked him down. He was dazed for a couple of minutes. This was a 40-plus men's beer league, and he was pulling crap like that. Being a defender of the underdog, the little guy, that got me fired up. I made it my mission to teach him a lesson. You don't come into our league brand new and pull stuff like that. Not on my watch.

I couldn't just shout a bunch of bravado at this guy. That doesn't go very far; I'd just get branded a loudmouth. I'd have to take him to the ice. He could skate circles around me. He could fire a shot at me and knock me into next week. I had to be smart. One thing he did recognize, but didn't fully respect, was when someone wouldn't back away from him. Then he'd try to either go around, or more often right through. This is what I was counting on. I may not have had a fraction of his talent, but I rivaled him in size and strength. If I could get a hip or a shoulder into him, he was going down.

We got out on the ice together, and I watched carefully for my opportunity. It didn't take long. He came bombing through center ice, and I was backing up on him. He juked just for a half step, but then figured I'd move out of his way, so he just kept coming at me. I pivoted just a bit and hit the brakes.

We collided in spectacular fashion, and both went down hard. It was great. He was stunned for a second, and then immediately started looking around for the ref, wondering why he hadn't blown the whistle on me. The ref was just laughing, and said, "There's nothing there, that was just a train wreck!" One thing about our league: guys who fly above the radar get noticed quickly by the refs and other players. If they get a bad reputation, the calls start going against them. That's what happened to this guy.

We encountered each other a few more times like that. He developed a grudging respect for me, and I laid off him a bit. Especially when the whistles started blowing in his favor and I'd end up in the penalty box.

Our final encounter was pretty rough, and completely an accident. In most contact sports, it's a good idea to keep your head on a swivel, to spot any opponents coming at you. In this case, we both had our heads on swivels – looking for the puck that was scooting around loose. In close proximity, we both turned right into each other, completely unaware of the other's presence.

It was a hard collision, stunning each of us, and we both went down. Unfortunately, he twisted and landed wrong on his back. He was hurt pretty bad and ended up needing surgery. Even though it was completely an accident, I felt bad and backed off on the physical play. He healed up and came back the next year. I toned it way, *way* down when we were on the ice together after that.

As Tammy wrapped up her degree and graduated in the spring of 1993, I started college full time at Ferris that fall, just a month or so after we got married and settled as a family. Tammy worked, doing both daycare and coaching community recreation gymnastics classes while I studied. We moved again, just a few blocks away into rental house – a full house, no pun intended. No more noisy apartments, we had the whole place to ourselves. And just in time, too. In the midst of my studies; in fact, while studying for my Calculus final, our daughter Kelly was born on July 3rd, 1995.

The birth was not without issue. Kelly had the umbilical cord wrapped around her neck, and the doctor was working to free her. It was one of the most stressful times of my life – Kelly's vital signs dipped low at least once and they had to move Tammy around significantly to get a better angle on Kelly. So, it was not only my first biological child being born, but under stress and trauma to boot.

I was a wreck. I left the delivery room at one point to go sit with Tammy's dad in the waiting room. They called me back in as Kelly was about to be delivered. The doctors must have thought I was a jerk for leaving, but I didn't know what to do. To say I was overloaded in the moment would be an understatement. But when I got back to the delivery room and the doctor had finished coaxing Kelly into the world, all the stress and chaos was forgotten. What an astounding miracle. I literally counted all of her fingers and toes in a vain effort to ensure she was whole and complete. My daughter was born, and I was a dad…again.

About that Calculus final: I had been on my way to a B+ in the class, but my studying was interrupted for obvious reasons. I ended up with a C due to the failed final. But it didn't matter. I passed the class, and my baby girl was born, in good health and in one piece.

We were nomads during this early time in our lives, and we moved one more time to a temporary residence. We moved into our fourth location since the original noisy apartment. Tammy had started Big Rapids Gymnastics, and I was still going to school full time at Ferris, so we found a house for rent in Big Rapids. It was during this stay that I graduated and landed a full-time job as a manufacturing engineer back at Nartron. Both of our college careers complete, we settled into the next stage of family life – working and raising the kids. And, Tammy would become pregnant again, with our son Matt.

Unfortunately, the fourth place we called home was cut shorter than expected when the owners put the house up for sale. With nowhere else to go, Tammy's parents offered us half of their house, so we moved our now five-member mob in with them. Their house was a big old affair, and was divided into an ad hoc two-family setup. Matt was born in January of 1998 during what was a crowded and stressful time of my life. As it turned out, Matt had ASD, and fairly significantly, which we would realize more over the next few years. Initially, it made him fussy and almost colicky as a baby, and this stressed me out. Hello, ASD sensory issues were back.

The main bathroom at the in-law's place was on our side of the house, and it had the washer and dryer in it. Along with the bathroom we had a living room, and three bedrooms upstairs. I would be in the living room, watching TV, trying to get Matt to relax, and Tammy's mom would come over to run laundry at any given time. I get it, laundry needs done, but this was a disruption to both mine and Matt's routines. We both craved peace and quiet. It was a long year.

When Matt was a year or so old, we finally bought our first house. No more nomadic lifestyle, no more rentals or in-laws. Back to Big Rapids, to Waterloo Street, a cute four-bedroom Cape Cod house. It had a huge double-sized back yard, and – the crown jewel – an in-ground pool.

We loved it there, and our family life really took off in that house. In the summers, I'd come home from work, change into swim trunks, and go out to the pool. I'd take time to clean it and maintain the chemical levels, and then...paradise. I'd jump in the deep end and just float for a few seconds under the water. It wasn't heated, but that was fine. It got warm enough in the summer, and I didn't want bathwater – that's not refreshing after a long day at work. I'd swim a couple of laps, then come out and just chill by the poolside for about 15-20 minutes.

I continued working at Nartron as an engineer, and Tammy continued both expanding her daycare up to a capacity of twelve children. We built a big swing & play set for the back yard, and put an egress window in the basement, which was partially finished. She was also running and coaching at Big Rapids Gymnastics. We were doing well. We were young, energetic, and motivated to make a good life for ourselves.

One characteristic I had (still have, actually) is the sense of taking things personally. It was borne out of the teasing and bullying during childhood, which was directly a result of my ASD awkwardness. So, directly or indirectly, my ASD causes me to take things the wrong way sometimes. Someone might be venting, upset at something in their world, and it'll have nothing to do with me. But if I cross their path, and say something tone-deaf to them – which people with Asperger's tend to do – then I'm likely to get a shot taken at me. And since I didn't perceive any offense on my part, I'll be a little thin-skinned about it. In my mind, they just attacked me for no apparent reason.

This can happen with things said to me even without an accidental offense. It's stems from a lack of proper social perception, a given for those on the spectrum. And it comes from a very strong sense of justice. Treating people fairly. Rooting for the underdog. It sucks to get mistreated, and I developed a strong attitude about it. That meant if someone did or said something that was just them lashing out, or misbehaving, I took it as a personal attack. "Why?? Why would you say that to me? Why would you do that? How could you!?"

Shortly after moving into our house, we took stock of our family. Four kids, all healthy and doing well. Troy was eleven, Terry eight, Kelly about four and a half, and Matt was not quite a year old. At this point, we thought it was a good idea to nip things in the bud, so to speak. So, I made an appointment to get a vasectomy.

The procedure was going along, and then the doctor seemed a little surprised at something. I kept calm and figured if it was a big deal, he'd say something. He got things under control (I guess), and I didn't hear any more exclamations. We wrapped up and before long I was up and hobbling out to my car.

Most men have their vasectomies on a Friday, recover from them over the weekend, and are back to work and normal activity by Monday. After two long, painful weeks, I was starting to get back to some semblance of normal. After another week, I was mostly back to normal. I didn't know, I'd obviously never had one of these procedures before, so I figured I must've just had a "bad reaction" to it. Or, how some people heal quicker than others from surgery or injuries, everything seemed to be going along fine. And then, a BIG surprise came out of nowhere in late 1999.

In October of that year, Tammy found out that she was pregnant. Again. I was floored. How could that be? Things had been back to normal for months now, and nothing. And then, all of a sudden...? It didn't make any sense. I called my doctor to set up an appointment to go in and get checked. He was very nervous and stumbling over his words. I was indeed still able to father children, and so it was not divine conception that caused Tammy to be with our fifth child.

I scheduled an appointment with a specialist in Grand Rapids. He went back in and made things right. But we saw Laura, our newest little bundle of joy-to-be, as an unexpected gift from God.

What came next was no gift, though. No sooner had we recovered from the news that we would be newborn parents yet again, that I received a letter in the mail over Thanksgiving weekend. It was a pink slip from Nartron. I had been laid off, again. Only this time there would be no going back.

I was crushed. I felt completely defeated. This wasn't fair. We were unexpectedly pregnant with our fifth child, and now my job gets cut out from under me with a "Dear John" letter. Over the holiday weekend, no less! The next Sunday at church, when the pastor called anyone needing prayer to step forward, I went up front. As soon as I started to explain my situation to the pastor, I just broke down. Talk about sensory overload. It all just hit home in that moment.

But when life hands us lemons, God gives us the sugar to make lemonade. To paraphrase a verse from 1st Corinthians chapter 10: He won't give us more than we can handle…as long as we walk with Him. And handle it, we did. I was working again within a few weeks, and Tammy's combination of daycare and gymnastics businesses kept us more than afloat. God is good, all the time.

As I look back now, I remember kind of an odd habit of mine at family functions. Tammy's side of the family is big, and they like to get together and visit, mostly on holidays and during the annual reunion. But still, there were always plenty of times throughout the year that some amount of her family would get together, and even part of it was still quite a few people. Sometimes it was at her grandparent's house and sometimes at her mom and dad's. But one thing that struck me, looking back, is how quiet and even uncomfortable I felt sitting with the adults in conversation.

Where I found myself most often was hanging out with Tammy's younger cousins, and even the kids. As the kids got a little older, I was most often playing euchre with them. I just didn't like to socialize much, at least with people my age or older. To me, it was boring to sit around and talk, and I felt out of place. It was much more fun, and I felt more at home, when I was hanging around with the younger crowd.

If you think about it from an ASD standpoint, it makes perfect sense. We are socially and emotionally under-developed; we tend to have a more childlike, even immature nature. For the longest time, and even still a bit today, I have hated the thought of getting older. I mean, I wanted to remain young, energetic and playful for as long as possible. A lot of that was for the kids' sake. I wanted to be there with them and enjoy their energy as much and as long as possible. I didn't want to "grow up" and be like those boring, stuffy adults that I felt out of place trying to relate to. The inability to socialize with others in my peer group goes back to the mind blindness explained in chapter 1. I don't have the ability to understand the nuances of facial expressions, body language, or even some verbal cues.

When the kids and cousins were younger, it was great, because kids aren't about nuance. They're pretty direct. There's not a lot of hidden meaning to their intentions. However, as my kids grew into teenagers, this opened up a whole new can of worms.

As parents, many of us look back at how we were raised. If we had siblings, we took note of the differences in how we were treated compared to them. Specifically, how we may have been treated lesser than them. With that in mind, we make a well-intentioned but doomed-to-fail vow to treat our own kids just the same. No favoritism in this house, no way.

And when they're little, it's actually pretty easy to do. Little kids are great – they're playful, loveable, and even when they act up, you can't stay angry for long at all. Even with my stress and sensory issues, I usually calmed down quickly if I got upset with them.

Each child is as unique as their fingerprints, and so too is their behavior. And as they grow, these differences in personality and behavior really start to develop. Thus, how we react to and treat each one individually will naturally be different. And there goes the fairness doctrine, right out the window.

The nature of ASD is to be more self-absorbed. As I explained in chapter 1, many neurodiverse people who are higher functioning want to be social and make friends, to have relationships. But socialization for an ASD individual is very difficult and creates anxiety. So, we tend to focus on our own interests, commandeering conversations so that others struggle to get a word in edgewise. While we're not consciously being arrogant or narcissistic, it can easily come across that way.

When children are younger, up to about middle school age, this isn't a huge problem. But now, imagine mixing this isolating self-absorption with a teenager, who think they know everything, and you've got a recipe for trouble.

The oldest, Troy, was very headstrong. He loved to debate. It was hard for him to take an answer or directive from us straightaway. He often negotiated things into his terms. He was very confident in his opinions. When he questioned, he knew the answer he was looking for. He was outgoing and friendly. While his stubbornness got in his way sometimes, he had no shortage of friends.

We had our differences, but in the end we got along, and even had a little fun along the way. He's the kind of person who can sell ice to an Eskimo. He played hockey for years, then switched to weightlifting. He became a very formidable bouncer, has run security teams at grand opening events and even a huge outdoor music festival. Whatever he does, he goes after it with gusto and puts his heart into it.

Terry, the second oldest, was about as opposite of Troy as you could get. Quiet and bookish, he rarely spoke up, much less talked back. He kept to himself a lot, and still does. Terry's very smart and loves to read. When he's motivated, he can learn about anything. Terry is always searching, seeking.

He's very easygoing, and tries to leave the smallest footprint possible. He's a very kind and caring individual. For as quiet and unassuming as Terry is, he did have a penchant for boxing and MMA fighting. Not just watching, but doing. A few years back, he got into serious training and had a single MMA cage bout. And he won, early in the second round. Not a bad way to retire, 1-0, undefeated.

Kelly, the oldest daughter and third in line, was also pretty quiet. It was hard (and still is) to get her to open up about much. She is determined and diligent. She helps run Tammy's gymnastics club, coaching a lot of kids, and taking on more responsibilities each year. She and Tammy are a pretty tight team.

She can speak up when she needs to; she's no pushover. She stuck up for kids who were bullied. She was a gymnast until about her freshman year of high school, then got into volleyball and track. She's always been athletic and strong, a lot like her aunt Becky. She makes a reserved but powerful leader for the kids.

Matt, the fourth in line and youngest son, is an interesting mix. He's also on the spectrum. We noticed his language was different between ages two and three. He was diagnosed by age three, and enrolled him in various therapies to help him deal with his neurodivergence at an early age. We moved from Big Rapids to Zeeland to get Matt into a school that focuses in special education needs for kids with cognitive impairments, including ASD. Matt was only there for one year of preschool, but they worked wonders with him.

Matt did karate and Tae kwon do from age ten until just last year. He went on to a regular school for kindergarten through eighth grade. After high school he went to college for a short time, but he wasn't sure the school or the program was right for him. He's currently working full time and exploring his options for getting into ministry.

Last but not least is Laura, our little surprise. She was a bundle of joy, always happy and smiling when she was little. She's got a big heart. Laura was also a gymnast until about age fourteen. Her strong will and physique make her a determined and accomplished athlete, too.

Driven to succeed, her grade point in high school was at least a 4.0. She's done very well in her first two and a half years of college. She's still trying to figure out what she wants to do. Once she settles in, though, she'll do very well.

"Having then gifts differing according to the grace that is given to us, let us use them..." Romans 12:6

PART 5: TESTED, AND LIFE MOVING FORWARD

8
LITTLE DID I KNOW

As each of these little fingerprints grew into the unique individuals that they are, I met each one as best I could, but of course it's never quite enough. It's the age-old dilemma; looking at the shortcomings of our own childhoods, we vow and strive to do better by our kids than our parents did. We want so much to not make the same mistakes; and, maybe we don't make the same ones. But we do make mistakes, and we have regrets. We look back and wish we'd been more patient, more loving, less uptight. This is a difficult thing for me to take.

I've almost had a phobia or an obsession about not looking back to the past, only forward. You can't change the past, so why dwell on it? I was in a situation not that long ago that briefly, but very strongly, brought memories back of when we were a young family. And it hit me hard. Gut tight, eyes watering. It just hit me like a tidal wave, and my reaction was…remorse, regret that I hadn't done a better job of raising my kids.

There's been some tension and distance with a couple of them, and it goes back to when they were in high school. But these memories went even farther back. From when they were little, and we were in our first house in Big Rapids, around that era. And the perfectionist in me, the part of me that feels like I screw things up and can't get them right, wanted so bad to go back in time and start over, right there on Waterloo Street, back when our oldest was only twelve and our youngest was just born.

If I could go back knowing then what I know now about this thing called ASD, and that I had it, and how it's affected me every step of the way since I was born, I would definitely do things differently. But I didn't know, and I can't go back. So, I have to make the best of what I've got moving forward.

As the kids grew through their respective teenage years, each had their own struggles, and I along with them. Troy was the first, and probably the hardest. He went through a tough time during his junior and senior years of high school. And I didn't deal with it well. We were often at odds. I just couldn't handle the disruption to the household rules. A lot of it was the ASD kicking in, as far as the intensity of my reactions, but I didn't know that at the time. He ended up moving out to live with his grandmother for a few months.

And then, after high school, he left Michigan altogether. Giving in to a flight of fancy, he boarded an Amtrak train bound for Los Angeles. No plans, nothing much with him except some cash and a bag of clothes. Some close friends of ours had a couple of their daughters living out there. They took him in and helped him get settled. And he loved it out there. It was just the release he needed. Thankfully, we've been able to mend things and we get along now better than ever.

Terry was less dramatic through his teenage and post-high school years. Quiet but firm in his beliefs, he marched to the beat of a different drummer. While he was outwardly more compliant, he yearned for independence and to be his own person. He lived with us for a few years after high school. But, in his early twenties and right after our latest move into our current home, he decided it was time to strike out on his own. Like I said, nothing dramatic, like hopping a train to the west coast; he just simply arranged an apartment downtown with a couple of his friends, and off he went. I was happy that he was becoming an independent young adult.

Kelly and I had some minor dustups. Her quiet simmer had found some boiling points. And I didn't react well to some of her situations. There was nothing wrong that she had done; far from it. I just wasn't there for her as a supportive father should've been. She takes things hard, like her dad, and my poor reactions to some situations created a rift between us. We're better now, but I know there's still some distance there – more than I'd like there to be.

Matt was a pretty chill kid through high school. He did have a major disagreement with our choice of high school for him. He wanted to go to the big public school where a lot of his friends from middle school went, but we sent him to a smaller private school instead. It was really the better choice for his education and maturity level. He tested out his rebelliousness from time to time, but never overdid it. By the time Matt was of age, I had learned how to handle things with teens…or so I thought.

When Laura hit her mid-teens, the fireworks flew between us. We got in some pretty big arguments. I think my shortcomings in dealing with both Kelly and Laura were mainly my unfamiliarity and inability in dealing with girls. My narrow line of thinking allows me to relate to what (and who) I know best. And that's guys. This was why I didn't relate well to Kelly when she needed me to, and this was why sparks flew between Laura and I when she'd speak up. She was the youngest, but she was most like her oldest brother; headstrong and not afraid to speak her mind.

And it was during some of these later battles, when she was in her last couple of years of high school, that finally clued Tammy into the fact that something might be going on with me besides just a short temper. Tammy later said she had noticed things in my behavior in the past, but it became more evident whenever Laura and I engaged. I've always had a strong sense of right and wrong, of perceived injustice, as far as my acting out. I didn't just root for the underdog, I often felt like I *was* the underdog. Any time the opportunity presented itself, I would encourage and help out anyone getting the short end of the stick. So, I reacted in kind whenever I felt that I was unfairly under attack; *I* was now the underdog in need of help. And so, I became very defensive in the heat of the moment. I did not hear what was being said to me with a father's care. I heard what was being thrown at me with a combatant's resistance.

In a moment of calm and reason, Tammy talked with me first about the idea that I might be exhibiting similar traits to what Matt experienced when he was younger. When I seemed agreeable to this, she then prompted me to try taking an online test, the Autism Quotient exam. It's made up of fifty questions, and gives the taker a rough idea of whether or not they're on the spectrum. When completed, the screen shows your score, there's a statement that reads "Scores in the 33-50 range indicate significant Autistic traits (Autism)." The two times I've taken this test, I've scored a 36 and 37, respectively.

From there, she led us to a clinical psychologist who specialized in spectrum and cognitive disorders. I didn't realize her specialty at first, and I was reluctant at first because I thought that both Laura and I were going, since I figured this was still in response to the flare-ups between us, and she needed to learn how to deal with conflict too. I began to realize that these counseling sessions were for me; well, rather, for Tammy and I. And I've come to understand that now. As the parents, the adults, it's our responsibility to sort out communications issues between us, and also with our children. (it's easy to say; it's another thing altogether to do, and do well, for that matter.)

After a few sessions of the good doctor verbally poking and prodding into our family, my work, etc. to gauge my condition, she administered her own test to me. This one was longer and more complex – the Ritvo Asperger Diagnostic Scale-Revised (or RAADS-R for short). The RAADS-R is an eighty-question exam that takes a good amount of time and thought to complete, and even longer to properly score. As we were meeting once a week, it took the doctor two full weeks to come back with the results. And when she did, I don't think any of us, including her, were ready for what the test told us.

She started by explaining that the threshold score was 65. This means that a neurotypical person, someone *not* on the spectrum, should score 65 or less. She then explained that those who were on the spectrum but high-functioning (such as myself) generally score in the 80s, from her experience. She then revealed my score…which totaled 143.

She looked at me, mouth agape for a minute. She couldn't comprehend it. The person sitting in front of her was a fully functioning father and husband who suffered at most from being a bit too uptight, with too much stress and anxiety in his life. What the score said *should* be sitting there was a babbling nutball with a few screws loose. That's hyperbole, of course, but based on her reaction, the score and the person clearly did not match up.

The fact that I scored that high on the RAADS-R test and was there to deal with some communication and relationship issues seemed like a huge understatement, I think. She immediately turned her efforts to me and taught me techniques to deal with the stress and anxiety that arises with sudden disruptions to my schedule, or when interactions with others don't go as planned. Priority was the key – what was really important to worry about, and what could I let slide as no big deal? I'll give some more detail on this in the Final Note.

I now had crucial information about myself that was previously unknown. I'd lived my whole life as an aggregate of what these test scores reflected. I had suffered through a childhood of being a spaz, a geek, a freak who didn't function well socially, had few friends and that seemed to be dealt a losing hand. And, I had grown up and raised a family with all the dysfunction and neuroses that such a life produces. But sitting here, learning the underlying truth about myself...this gave me significant insight into who I was. And it gave insight into who I *could* be.

"For I know the thoughts that I think toward you, says the Lord, thoughts of peace and not of evil, to give you a future and a hope." Jeremiah 29:11

9
LIFE SINCE THE DIAGNOSIS

It's been just over two years since the counseling sessions and testing. Finding out that I have ASD has been a revelation. I remember right after that session with the counselor, where she revealed my score, I was home, thinking and taking stock of everything. I thought back on things and had light bulbs going off like crazy.

So many things made sense, back to early childhood, about why I acted and reacted the way I did. I just kept having flashback after flashback to different points in my life, different situations, from toddler age up to just a handful of years ago. I thought of it as a conscious, low-stress Life Review Experience. That's the scientific term for having your life flash before your eyes. It was like a slow-motion version, where different scenes of my life would play back one or maybe a few at a time, over a number of days.

It's been a double-edged sword, knowing. As I think about it, though, the benefits far outweigh the disadvantages. In fact, I'll start with the disadvantages, or the one big one that I worried about from the beginning. That is, that I would lean on my new knowledge as a "label," and use it as a crutch to excuse negative behavior that I might otherwise control. I've made it this far in life, no need to consider myself disabled now.

Another one that may or may not be related to ASD is that I've really backed off of life and engaging. I've always charged ahead, taking on any challenge, having a real fighting attitude – in more ways than one. I haven't been as hard-charging over the last few years. This one, honestly, is probably as much due to age as anything else. I am fifty-four, after all, and while I'm still in good shape, I think the mid-fifties is a typical slow-down time for a lot of people. So that one I'll count as secondary, or indirect.

Another con related to the last one is a feeling of weariness. I'm weary of disagreements. I tend to get very defensive and feel like I'm being made to feel not just wrong, but that I'm a bad person.

It's a vicious circle. People on the spectrum tend to get defensive because in the past they've been rejected and even persecuted for what they are and how they perceive and react. So, when someone challenges our point of view in what might be a normal, everyday disagreement, that old self-preserving defensiveness rises up. We're fiercely independent for two reasons; one, it's just our nature to be solitary, since social discomfort is typically our number one trait. And two, we've learned to take care of ourselves. After being viewed as odd, weird, and called that and worse throughout our lives, we've turned inward for support and validation.

And again, don't get me wrong, most people with Asperger's want very much to have friends, and even be close to a special someone. But the act of doing that goes against our nature – the way our brains are wired, we don't understand socializing and it makes us very uncomfortable. Over time we learn tricks to mask and cope and get along without much stress. But it still takes us a separate effort, consciously learned over time, to do something that comes naturally to the neurotypical world.

When you're masking, coping, camouflaging (pick your term), you're making a separate effort to be something you're not. You're being unnatural to yourself, to put it bluntly, and that takes a toll. It takes mental and emotional energy to keep up an appearance that isn't part of our natural selves. We get fatigued, hence burnout and meltdowns. Our brains are still that one-track freight train, barreling along down a given path. One of the other things many of us have learned as a masking or coping mechanism is to artificially slow the train. I think of it as "dumbing down" our train of thought. For a long time, it anguished me to think about it and realize what I was doing. I was torn between what I needed to do to get along better with others at work and at home, versus being myself.

For example, I love sitting and working math problems. Algebra, trigonometry, geometry, even calculus. I love it. They're like puzzles to me. But more than that, I get an extra sense of satisfaction from doing them because, for so long as a child, I was terrible at math and didn't get it at all until my early twenties. They're to me what a crossword or jigsaw puzzle might be to someone else. I'm at my natural best when I'm sitting and working math problems. Or, when I'm sitting and writing, either in my journal, an article or a book.

I love solitary activities that utilize my intellect. It's not that I don't like people or hate being around them, it's just that I can be completely comfortable by myself. I love my wife and love being around her. Our personalities are very different, though, and those differences can stress me to the point of needing a break. It's nothing she's done wrong, it's just who she is. Just as there's nothing wrong with how I'm put together, we're just different. And I think that she needs a break from me sometimes, too.

Finding out I have ASD this late in life created a bit of dichotomy in my psyche, and that can be tough to deal with. As I mentioned earlier, it can be a double-edged sword, knowing this sort of thing. On the one hand, I was glad to finally find out. It was a bit of a relief to discover that my adverse and even extreme reactions to different things over the years weren't just me being a spaz or a jerk. It was very cool to look back, have that low-pressure LRE and see it like finding the last few pieces of a puzzle as they fall into place at different points in my life. On the other hand, I don't want to revel in this newly identified condition. I don't want to celebrate a label that can be "used for evil," to make excuses for bad behavior.

As far as the benefits of knowing that I have ASD, even just finding out this late in life – well, there are several. For instance, a big one is being able to foresee trouble spots and trigger points ahead of time, before I get too stressed. I'm able to more calmly and clearly communicate them to Tammy or others. I can then choose to continue, or I can choose to avoid that situation altogether.

Another good thing – for me, anyway – is the pause it's given me for introspection. That's something I enjoy doing anyway, solitary thinking that leads to self-improvement. How can I deal with certain situations and relationships better than I have before? I run through techniques to help calm and focus my mind.

Similar to the introspection is that this knowledge has helped me look back and re-identify who I am. I've done a lot of masking – mimicking and masquerading – over the years in order to fit in and get along. Even though it's unnatural behavior and it takes effort to pull off, it has become a part of my normal daily mental wardrobe, if you will.

After years of doing this, it becomes easier and so it shapes not only how I act but how I think about myself. Sometimes I question my motives and desires, behaviors I had a few decades ago to now. Am I really okay with acting that way, or should I drop the act and just be myself, even though I'll come across as eccentric and even a bit nonsensical?

Many people need to exercise some conscious restraint in their natures at times to avoid creating an awkward or disruptive situation. However, it's a great relief to finally understand the totality of WHY I've had to do that, to the extent that I've had to, for so long (and still, to this day).

10
PERSPECTIVES

One thing that has helped me over the last couple of years is to dig in and research the topic of Asperger's, autism and ASD in general. Finding others who have ASD and learning their perspectives on situations helps a great deal. You realize you're not alone, and there are ways to deal with things that can be difficult.

I mentioned Paul Micallef in chapter 2 and his channel, "Aspergers from the Inside." Paul has some great insights on dealing with relationships, work stress, avoiding meltdowns, and so on. Look him up. If you've got a question or struggle, chances are Paul's done a video on it and has some great advice to offer.

Dan from The Aspie World is another good YouTube channel. Dan's got Asperger's, ADHD and dyslexia, so he knows what he's talking about when it comes to dealing with neurological conditions.

Another fellow "Aspergian" (to use his term) is someone I learned about while watching one of Paul's videos. John Elder Robison wrote his memoir, entitled "Look Me in the Eye," and Paul had recommended it as a must-read. I bought the book, and couldn't put it down. I read it, from beginning to end, within a week. He has some amazing stories – the truth really can be stranger than fiction!

One thing John noticed is how later in life the brain can rewire itself. When he was young, from his teenage years through his twenties, he was an expert in electronics. Strictly self-taught, he worked in the music industry repairing and modifying amplifiers and other sound equipment. He could not only design his own circuits, but he could even envision ahead of time the type of sound they would produce.

After spending years in the music industry, he moved into creating electronic games with Milton Bradley. They moved him up the ladder fast, and before long he was director of his department. He found that corporate life didn't suit him, so he left electronics behind and got into cars, another love of his from childhood. He was proficient at mechanical repair as a boy, but later in life, after burning out of the corporate world, he really threw himself at learning how to repair and restore Bentleys, Land Rovers, Jaguars and other high-end cars. He opened his own service shop and still runs J.E. Robison Service Co. in Springfield, Massachusetts.

He noted in his memoir that, at age fifty and a successful exotic car enthusiast, he looked back at his early work in electronics. He said he would look at some of the circuits he designed and built, and it was like looking at someone else's work. He said he no longer understood how the circuits worked, and that he wouldn't be able to build them today. His focus had shifted over the years to mechanical automobile repair, and away from complex electronic circuitry. In his thinking, his brain had rewired itself for automobile repair.

That's true, if you think about it: your brain is like a muscle, and the different areas that support different talents and abilities need to be exercised through practice of those abilities. Like playing music, or learning mathematics. If you practice, you get better. If you stop practicing and performing altogether, that part of the brain's "muscle" will atrophy and you can lose the ability.

My dad had told me to never stop learning, so I don't. I've learned more about car repair in the last few years than ever before. I took a keen interest in acquiring a decent tool collection and trying my hand at various repairs. Having the right tool for the job can make the difference between getting a job done quickly and easily, or spending hours muttering and throwing wrenches across the garage. I've done oil changes and brake jobs for a long time. But more recently I've done front suspension work, and replaced various sensors. I've removed intake manifolds and throttle bodies.

I've also found that when your child gets in a minor fender bender, replacing the front fascia and other exterior panels of the car is really not that difficult. I've rebuilt the front of Kelly's car, my car, and Matt's car twice. Once after he hit a deer, and more recently after someone ran into him. I can't do extensive structural repair, but if it's mostly superficial, no problem. Transmission and drivetrain service, as far as fluid changes, are doable.

I started this years ago, with the oil and brake pad changes, to save money. I figured that, the shop would charge me a couple hundred bucks minimum to change my brake pads and rotors, or I could simply buy the parts for $100 and spend an hour or so in the garage. In the case of the minor fender benders, body work is very expensive – probably $1,000 minimum to do what I have done for $200 in parts. It's not as refined and professional, but it's close enough and no one will know the difference.

It's challenging. It's even fun…when I don't encounter the repair from hell that leaves me hours in the garage with little to show for it, wondering why I even got out of bed that day. More than once, I've had to take the car to my mechanic when I'd messed something up. But I keep doing, and learning. You're never too old to learn and try something new.

A FINAL NOTE

If you, or someone you know, may be exhibiting behavior that appears to be short-tempered, or they seem to "melt down" at the slightest thing, look into ASD and see if the criteria fit the condition. Some people may be defensive and think you're trying to find something wrong with them. As defensive as I had been earlier on, Tammy's gentle, stepped approach helped break the ice and got me to take that first Autism Quotient test online. It also helped that one of our kids is on the spectrum, so the idea wasn't strange or unknown to me.

As I mentioned toward the end of chapter 8, the counselor helped me by giving me some exercises that can help ward off an overload situation. These are simple but effective techniques that anyone, on the spectrum or not, can use. You may have used them before.

Number one: breathe, and count to ten. Simple yet effective. Make a conscious effort to clear your mind while breathing and counting. This helps relieve the initial spark of stress.

Number two: prioritizing. She recommended taking a moment to list the different activities that are piled up. I write them on a piece of paper; it helps slow my brain down and gives me a clear visual of what I'm dealing with. Then decide which are critical and which aren't. For example, during the summer I wanted to spend a good amount of a particular day writing, but I also had to work on one of the cars. Then my wife interjected with doing something with the family. I was stressed because my schedule was thrown off with an unforeseen addition.

Instead of going off into overload mode, I stop and breathe, count to ten, and then slowly and deliberately think through the day's agenda. What *needs* to be done, and what can be put off until later, or tomorrow? This gives me the opportunity to make decisions and provide input into the schedule, while lightening the load at the same time. The oil change ended up waiting until the next day, I got some writing done, and we had a good time with the kids over for dinner and cards.

Another thing to look into is your personality type. I mentioned this briefly in chapter 2. Being an introvert, engaging in introspection and analyzing thoughts and actions comes naturally to me anyway. But there are other naturally occurring behaviors, attitudes and beliefs that are part of who I am aside from the Asperger's.

I highly recommend checking out these two books: *Gifts Differing* by Isabel Briggs Myers and *Please Understand Me II* by David Keirsey. Myers-Briggs is a premiere expert and resource on personality typing. With the help of her mother, they researched the famous psychologist Carl Jung's work on psychological typing from the 1920s and wanted to make it accessible to the general public.

In 1962, they launched the Myers-Briggs Type Indicator (MBTI), a questionnaire that categorized a person's personality type into one of four main categories. There were four sub-categories within each, and with the results of the indicator, a person could then see and understand his or her natural strengths and weaknesses; inclinations and aversions.

David Keirsey, a fan of Myers-Briggs' work, sought to make personality typing even more user-friendly for people. To use a math analogy: Carl Jung's work from the 1920s is the calculus of personality types. Myers-Briggs has brought it down to trigonometry, and Keirsey has provided a system akin to basic algebra. In his book, he offers the Keirsey Temperament Sorter II, his own questionnaire that leads the taker to one of sixteen different personality types, one of four subsets within each of four main categories.

All that being said, my personality type goes back and forth between INFJ and INFP. The "I" means Introvert, the "N" for iNtuitive thinker, the "F" means I make decisions based on Feelings rather than thinking, and the "J" and "P" are the difference between how decisive I am at a given time. Js (Judging) are disciplined to get things decided. They can quickly and easily can make a clear decision with logic. Ps (Perceiving) look at situations and decisions based on principles. That is, they are willing to let things go for a bit, see what comes up. They're more free-spirited than the Js.

This is interesting because I know my true nature is to base my thinking and decisions based on principle. I am literally often saying, to others or to myself, "It's the PRINCIPLE of the thing." As far as being free-spirited, I think my family might chuckle and look twice at that one. I've been anything but carefree throughout my life. Well, correction. I've been rarely carefree.

Again, I know it's in there and I know it's my natural best, but Asperger's forces certain habits and behaviors, and my work in quality engineering has led me to become more logical and decisive. I really do love being easygoing, and engaging in broader thinking based on principles and ideas, but structure and schedule are needed for my ND brain and work, and it causes me to be more rigid at times.

That's my story. All I hope for is that this helps someone who's struggled into their adult life feeling stress and anxiety where others don't; who've felt like an outcast and, as much as they may want to, can't socialize well and aren't comfortable with it. There are other traits that are indicative of spectrum disorder, so do some homework and see if they line up with your personality or the personality of someone you know and love.

"Before I formed you in the womb I knew you; Before you were born I sanctified you..." Jeremiah 1:5

www.ingramcontent.com/pod-product-compliance
Lightning Source LLC
Chambersburg PA
CBHW071818020426
42331CB00007B/1531